The

SODOMY

of

CHRISTIANS

The Biblical View

Martin & Deidre Bobgan

Unless otherwise indicated, Scripture quotations are taken from the Authorized King James Version of the Bible

The Sodomy of Christians
The Biblical View

Copyright © 2017 Martin and Deidre Bobgan
Published by EastGate Publishers
4137 Primavera Road
Santa Barbara, CA 93110

Library of Congress Control Number: 2017916346
ISBN 978-0941717-25-0

This I say therefore, and testify in the Lord, that ye henceforth walk not as other Gentiles walk, in the vanity of their mind....

That ye put off concerning the former conversation the old man, which is corrupt according to the deceitful lusts;

And be renewed in the spirit of your mind;

And that ye put on the new man, which after God is created in righteousness and true holiness.

Ephesians 4:17, 22-24

Visit
www.pamweb.org/mainpage.html
for
free ebooks, articles,
and video links

Contents

Introduction

The Sodomy of Christians: The Biblical View **(hereafter referred to as *SOC*) is written for Christians who desire to think and live according to the Word of God, because many, perhaps unknowingly, are following the sinful ways of the world in the marriage bed.** We provide information about the sexual climate in America and in the church to alert Christians to the dangers of sodomy and to urge all Christians to discipline their bodies according to God's sexual design for mankind as revealed in Scripture. Christians who have engaged in sexual intimacy outside the pattern of God's design, as clearly revealed in Scripture, need to follow the Narrow Way, rather than the ways of the world, the flesh, and the devil

We have three purposes in mind for which we provide ample biblical and practical support. **First and foremost of importance is to explain God's sexual design for mankind, which is sexual intercourse within the covenant of marriage between one man and one woman.** The second purpose is to reveal that the adoption and practice of oral and anal sex by many Americans, including Christians, was the cataclysmic catalyst that preceded and enabled America to embrace the whole homosexual agenda! The third purpose is to show that the growing practice and promotion of oral and anal sex among Christians is a dishonorable and vile violation of God's sexual design for sexual intercourse.

While it sounds redundant, *SOC* is about the sodomy of Christians. A legal dictionary defines *sodomy* as follows: "*Sodomy* refers to anal or oral sex, whether between a man and a woman, two women, or two men."[1] To put it bluntly, *SOC* is about oral and anal sex being practiced by many Christians and how this came to be. We describe how and why, in recent history, many Christians moved from orthodox (sound doctrine) biblical beliefs about sexuality to the outright acceptance of oral and anal sex. This unbiblical, latter-day reversal in belief was made possible when many in the church began participating in sodomy: oral and anal sex.

The title of this book may sound extreme. However, since the sexual revolution of the 1960s taking off, gaining speed through the last half of the Twentieth Century, and coming to full flower in the Twenty-First Century, many Americans and Christians have become compromised or undecided about the homosexual agenda. **In *SOC* we reveal that the sensual and sinful pleasures of oral and anal sex have seduced many Americans and Christians into embracing this ungodly behavior, contrary and contradictory to God's design for human sexuality.** We also reveal how this dramatic change occurred and why such practices became acceptable to many in America and in the church, which led to the acceptance of the entire homosexual agenda. **The reason

why Americans and many Christians have swallowed the whole homosexual agenda is because many heterosexual Americans and Christians were themselves practicing homosexual sexual acts. After all, aside from the gender of their partners, heterosexuals were doing the same thing as homosexuals: oral and anal sex.

In *SOC* we plainly present the biblical view of human sexuality and sexual intercourse. In addition, we bluntly discuss two of the many sexual acts of homosexuals and how these acts have influenced society as a whole, individual Christians, and the Church. **We issue a caveat to those who would be sensitive to the terms used as we clearly describe sexual intercourse according to the Bible and as we candidly describe oral and anal sex.** Throughout this book we report on surveys and research to support what we say, but **the Bible is the true and final Word that supersedes all surveys and research.**

Chapters 1-8

In Chapter 1, "God's Sexual Design," we present the orthodox biblical view of human sexuality. God created man and woman in such a way as to enable them to connect with one another organically and relationally as one flesh. Thus, according to God's purpose and design, human sexuality is between one man and one woman in a committed relationship for procreation and for pleasurable intimacy. In Chapter 2 we describe the orthodox biblical view of like-sex relationships and homosexual sexual practices, which, according to the Bible, are offenses against God, His Word, and His creation.

In Chapter 3, we give an overview of "The Sexual Revolution" and its impact on changing attitudes towards homosexual sexual practices and concomitantly on infl - encing the response of the country and the church. The sexual revolution in America was the cauldron within which "The Sodomy of Americans" (Chapter 4) evolved into the acceptance of homosexuals as a minority group with special minority-group rights along with their homosexual practices. During this time, the sodomy of Americans, with their openness to all forms of sexual practices between homosexuals and some between heterosexuals, leached into the liberal churches and eventually into many of the conservative churches, which led to "The Sodomy of Christians" (Chapter 5).

Our concern is with two of the many homosexual sexual practices and their adoption by Americans and particularly by many professing Christians. **We are not blaming the homosexual community for the ungodly behavior of Christians, but rather appealing to Christians to follow God's design for human sexuality.** ***SOC* will hopefully be a biblical wake-up call to those Christians who are violating God's design for sexual intimacy by replicating the sexual sins of homosexuals.**

The Song of Solomon, also known as Song of Songs and Canticles, has been used by many Christian couples to support their involvement in oral sex. Therefore, we present The Song of Solomon in its traditional biblical understandings (Chapter 6). In Chapter 7, "Dangers and Diseases of Sodomy," we reveal the dangerous bodily hazards of oral and anal sex, whether indulged in by homosexuals or heterosexuals. Obviously, God wired into

His sexual design a penalty for those who rebel against Him in this area of sexual behavior. In Chapter 8, "Love God and Your Spouse," we issue a clarion call to Christians and the church to obey God in the area of sexuality and a plea to any Christian who is indulging in any one of the sinful, sometimes life-threatening homosexual practices to repent and then to cease and desist.

Disclaimers

We begin with some disclaimers. First, although we will be presenting what the Bible reveals about homosexuality and homosexual practices, our focus is not to confront the homosexual view of Scripture, which is of recent origin and contradicts the orthodox, established understanding of what the Bible says, because many other writers have so ably and excellently addressed this issue.[2] Second, we will not be attempting to evangelize homosexuals, as there are many books that competently do so. Instead, we are writing to and for Christians who believe in the authority and sufficiency of the Bible. Third, except for brief references, we will not be saying much on the transgender issue, because that is a subject for another book. We have published an article on the transgender issue, which is available at our website.[3]

Changes in Sexual Perceptions and Practices

Homosexual sexual practices have been on the rise in the world, in the church, and among many of those who call themselves Christians. Many factors have been at work to bring about changes in the public attitude towards the sexual practices of homosexuals, such as affluence, belief in evolution, the Kinsey Reports, humanistic psychology, sociology, anthropology, and the media, which includes the visual and auditory means of communication and entertainment. **However, underneath all of this is mankind's rebellion against God and His creation. But even beyond the human rebellion is Satan's malevolent, malicious scheme to usurp God's reign and ruin His creation.** At all times, Christians need to remember that as believers we "wrestle not against flesh and blood, but against principalities, against powers, against the rulers of the darkness of this world, against spiritual wickedness in high places" (Eph. 6:12).

SOC is written for Christians who desire to think biblically about human sexuality as designed by our Creator. Every departure from male-female sexuality within the confines of marriage is in violation of God's design. He has clearly forbidden the same-sex practices of homosexuals. They are serious sinful acts calling for confession and repentance before God, not promotion and cries for acceptance in the public square or tacit acceptance within the family of God. Therefore, we simply present how the Bible has been traditionally understood regarding homosexual sexuality through numerous years of Bible scholarship, faithful teaching, and preaching and how the homosexual sexual practices of oral and anal sex violate God's sexual design for mankind.

The Bible is the Word of God and the infallible guide for living a life pleasing to God by grace through faith. And it is from this viewpoint that we examine present-day homosexual sexual practices coming into the marriage bed of Christian couples. Many in the church have been moving from the biblical truth about homosexuality and homosexual sexual practices, because they have been indulging in sodomy and justifying it with a misunderstanding of all that is included in making the marriage "bed undefiled" (Heb. 13:4). We will also reveal the behind-the-scenes dramatic changes in church circles that resulted in this tragedy.

Loving God and Others

Because of God's great love revealed in Christ's sacrificial death, resurrection, gift of new life, and ongoing intercession for all believers, we desire to follow Christ and to allow His life in us to influence all we say and do. God is love. He is the creator and initiator of love. "We love him, because he first loved us" (1 John 4:19). Therefore, as Christians we aspire to follow the Great Commandment:

> The first of all the commandments is, Hear, O Israel; The Lord our God is one Lord: And thou shalt love the Lord thy God with all thy heart, and with all thy soul, and with all thy mind, and with all thy strength: this is the first commandment. And the second is like, namely this, Thou shalt love thy neighbour as thyself. There is none other commandment greater than these. (Mark 12:29-31.)

Loving God involves knowing and walking according to His truth as revealed in the Bible and loving our neighbors in truth and love—speaking truth in love and mercy—not departing from God's truth while expressing God's love. This can be a hard call and it is easy to fall one way or the other if we do not maintain an inner vision focused on Jesus Himself. Therefore, as we dare approach the subject of homosexual sexual activities and their influence on the sexual behavior of many Americans and Christians, we must speak forth the truth of God in which we stand without departing from love and mercy as delineated in Scripture.

This book is written to encourage fellow believers to keep the faith without resorting to either capitulation or animosity. The primary message to all non-Christians should always be the Gospel of Jesus Christ. Thus we are to treat members of the homosexual community just as we would treat other unbelievers—kindly, fairly, and with the hope of winning them to Christ.

The primary message in *SOC* to all Christians is to live a life pleasing to God, which includes the area of sexuality. As Christians we must ever be as wise as serpents and as gentle as doves (Matt. 10:16) as we desire to follow Christ's prayer for us that, though we walk in the world, we do not live according to the ways of the world:

> I have given them thy word; and the world hath hated them, because they are not of the world, even as I am not of the world. I pray not that thou shouldest take them out of the world, but that thou shouldest keep them from the evil. They are not of the world, even as I am not of the world. Sanctify them through thy truth: thy word is truth. (John 17:14-17.)

Throughout this book we hope to encourage fellow Christians to follow the Word of God and therefore be set apart (sanctified) from the ways of the world, the flesh, and the devil. While rejecting sinful sexual practices, we must walk in love, which contains both mercy and truth.

We are not called to correct homosexuals, but to call Christians back to sexual purity in their own lives so that as believers we might all be true witnesses of Christ and thereby glorify God as the Creator and sustainer of human life and as the Father of the new life procured by Jesus Christ the Son, sustained by the Holy Spirit and nurtured by the Word of God.

God's Perfect Design

God's design for the marriage bed is under attack. Wanting people to be open to oral and anal sex, homosexual activists have hijacked the internet with false answers to true questions, such as the healthiest form of sex. The information in this book must be given to those Christians about to marry, those who have been married a short time, and those who have not waited until marriage. If oral and anal sex are not stopped before beginning or early on, they will dominate the marriage bed throughout the life of the marriage, as it will be extremely difficult to stop because of the intense pleasure given to the husband.

Most people know about oral and anal sex before marriage whether they are Christians or not. Therefore, they enter the marriage bed with this information. This is the time these two sodomy acts, to which we restrict ourselves in this book, are generally started. There are two reasons why neither oral nor anal sex should even be tried. The first reason is that God's perfect design for a godly couple in marriage is coital sex and all it involves, such as a wife's breasts and body, which are available for the pleasures of both husband and wife.

The **second** reason is that the healthiest of the sex acts is coital sex and not oral or anal sex, i.e. sodomy. The husband is the one who directs the sexual activity. **Because the husband is the head of the wife, God will hold the husband responsible for any sexual deviations from His perfect design of coital sex and all that involves.**

1

God's Sexual Design

God created human beings and their sexual relationships according to His perfect design. To gain a biblical perspective on sexual relationships and practices, we must begin at the very beginning. Instead of looking to human speculation about the beginning of humanity, we must turn to God's Word. He was there and He did it. The Bible clearly tells us: "In the beginning God created…man in his own image, in the image of God created he him, male and female created he them." Prior to this supreme act of creation, "God created the heaven and the earth" (Gen. 1:1, 27). God created all matter, energy, and time out of nothing. He formed the earth perfectly for the man who was to be made in His image: male and female.

> And God said, Let us make man in our image, after our likeness: and let them have dominion over the fish of the sea, and over the fowl of the air, and over the cattle, and over all the earth, and over every creeping thing that creepeth upon the

earth. So God created man in his own image, in the image of God created he him; male and female created he them. And God blessed them, and God said unto them, Be fruitful, and multiply, and replenish the earth, and subdue it: and have dominion over the fish of the sea, and over the fowl of the air, and over every living thing that moveth upon the earth. (Gen. 1:26-28.)

Notice how God uses both the singular "man" and the plural: "Male and female created He them."

The Beginning of Sexuality

Genesis 2 describes how God made one man into the plural: male and female. Yet the plural becomes one again as the man and woman join together physically and relationally for companionship, communication, intimacy, and procreation: "And the Lord God said, It is not good that the man should be alone; I will make him an help meet for him" (Gen. 2:18). Adam was created for relationship. Being made in the image of God meant that he had the capacity to love and be loved, just as God is love and has oneness in being Father, Son, and Holy Spirit. God's creation of man and woman therefore involves the capacity to give and receive love.

God formed Adam from the dust of the ground, but He formed the woman directly from the man. She received from his DNA with a major exception: XX rather than XY. Thus they were of the same flesh, complementary, but not identical. The woman is called a "help meet for him," which means a helping counterpart to the man. The differences between the man and woman are important in that they give one another some of what the other may be lacking. Even the brains are different in order to contribute to a whole (uniting of one man and one woman) that is greater than the sum of its parts. Two of the same would not provide the broader spectrum of abilities and thinking processes as two that are similar, but different and yet complementary.

Research on the brain highlights some of the overall, general differences between the brains of men and women. These differences begin before birth and continue throughout life. *Science News* reports:

> The reason boys like trucks and girls like dolls relates to fetal differences in brain development.... Males develop differently from females—physically and behaviorally— largely through programming by androgens (male sex hormones such as testosterone). [1]

Scientific American Mind reports differences in the neural networks of intelligence in men and women. They say:

> The specific areas in this network are different in men and women, suggesting there are at least two different brain architectures that produce equivalent performance on IQ tests. In general, we found that in women more gray and white matter in frontal brain areas, especially those associated with language, was correlated with IQ scores; in men IQ scores correlated with gray matter in frontal areas and, especially, in posterior areas that integrate sensory information. [2]

Of course there are similarities between the brains of men and women. However, *Scientific American Mind* says, "It turns out that male and female brains differ quite a bit in architecture and activity."[3] The journal also says that "over the past decade investigators have documented an astonishing array of structural, chemical and functional variations in the brains of males and females."[4]

Medical doctor Louann Brizendine, in her book *The Female Brain*, describes a woman as "a person whose reality dictated that communication, connection, emotional sensitivity, and responsiveness were the primary values."[5] Brizendine's theme throughout the book is that women are different because they have different brains, and, as a result, women are deeply sensitive to emotions and form strong relationships.

One writer sums it up by saying: "There is ample evidence that men and women think, express themselves and even experience emotions differently."[6] In addition to their brains, there are other bodily differences between males and females, such as hormonal differences. Even their sensory organs register differently. An article titled "5 Surprising Ways Men and Women Sense Things Differently" says:

> …studies suggest that women really do seem to be the more "sensitive gender." That is, they tend to taste, smell, hear, see colors, and feel textures more accurately than men—even though, in most cases, researchers aren't sure exactly why, says Marcia Pelchat, PhD, a sensory scientist who studies taste and smell at the Monell Chemical Sciences Center in Philadelphia.[7]

God created the man and the woman as complementary beings physically, mentally, emotionally, and procreationally.

Man and Woman Becoming One Flesh

The man and the woman need one another to be a complete unit for the purpose of mutual love, relationship, companionship, purpose, pleasure, and procreation: to fulfill God's plan for them to be "fruitful, and multiply, and replenish the earth, and subdue it: and have dominion...." Therefore, God made woman from man and established their sexual pattern of one man and one woman uniting as one flesh

> And the LORD God caused a deep sleep to fall upon Adam, and he slept: and he took one of his ribs, and closed up the flesh instead thereof; And the rib, which the LORD God had taken from man, made he a woman, and brought her unto the man. And Adam said, This is now bone of my bones, and flesh of my flesh: she shall be called Woman, because she was taken out of Man. Therefore shall a man leave his father and his mother, and shall cleave unto his wife: and they shall be one flesh. And they were both naked, the man and his wife, and were not ashamed. (Gen. 2:21-25.)

God's creation of the first man and woman was the amazing centerpiece of His universe. God breathed life into them and formed the depths of their souls in such a way as to reflect Him in many of His attributes. He formed them to be social beings, in which there would be mutual love, tenderness, care, purpose, and understanding. Their oneness included openness to one another and mutual care and love; their oneness was also physical. God formed them organically and sexually so that their oneness would be physical and sexual as well. Their pure nakedness identified their sexual identity in a clear and compelling way. **Thus the sexual union of one man and one woman was clearly established early in Genesis, and their sexual organs matched perfectly for becoming one flesh and being fruitful and multiplying.** The physical oneness of relationship is seen as the man's procreative organ enters the woman's reproductive organ, whereby they become one flesh. The man's sperm then penetrates the woman's ovum and another human being can be formed. Thus man and woman were made for each other to accomplish their God-given purpose: to love each other as one flesh (Eph. 5:25-33) and to bring forth new life to fill the earth (Genesis 1:26-28).

Even before there were fathers and mothers, **the pattern was set: one man plus one woman uniting as one flesh: one lasting union.** Adam clearly connected the fact that, just as Eve was created out of his own flesh, the relationship between them reflected their one flesh. He also confirmed God's design for one man and one woman to continue into the future when he said, "Therefore shall a man leave his father and his mother, and shall cleave unto his wife: and they shall be one flesh" (Gen 2:24). The union is one in which there is cleaving, staying together, not two people going their separate ways. Notice the importance of the sexual identification and the relationship between a man and a woman. God created sexual identification, relationship, purpose, and pleasure for uniting one man and one woman in an enduring relationship. The importance of this relationship is repeated throughout Scripture.

Jesus reminded his listeners of the Genesis of marriage between one man and one woman in Matthew 19 in answer to the Pharisee's question about divorce:

> Have ye not read, that he which made them at the beginning made them male and female, and said, For this cause shall a man leave father and mother, and shall cleave to his wife: and they twain shall be one flesh? Wherefore they are no more twain, but one flesh. What therefore God hath joined together, let not man put asunder. (Matt. 19:4-6.)

Thus the relationship was created to continue on within the marriage between one man and one woman. Although God allowed divorce specifically for the nation of Israel within the strict guidelines of the Mosaic law, Jesus declared: "Whosoever shall put away his wife, except it be for fornication, and shall marry another, committeth adultery: and whoso marrieth her which is put away doth commit adultery" (Matt. 19:9). The one flesh principle (one man joined with one woman) was from the beginning and continues to be God's will for mankind.

The Biblical pattern has been set. Just as one human became two (male and female) in creation, the two become one again sexually and organically. The physical coming together as one flesh happens when one man and one woman join together sexually according to God's design. Because this sexual coming together forms one flesh, Paul warned the Corinthians believers

> Know ye not that your bodies are the members of Christ? Shall I then take the members of Christ, and make them the members of an harlot? God forbid. What? Know ye not that he which is joined to an harlot is one body? For two, saith he, shall be one flesh. (1 Co . 6:15-16.)

In other words, if a Christian joins with someone sexually, he/she becomes one flesh with the other person and thereby involves Christ in the relationship.

The two coming together as one flesh is a sacred act, which should never be tampered with, either through adultery or any form of uncleanness or fornication. Moreover, because believers are in Christ and are to live by His life, their every act should be such that it honors God. **Marital fidelity is sacrosanct: extremely sacred and inviolable throughout Scripture. Therefore, conjugal faithfulness is mandated by God's Word.**

In his book *What Does the Bible Really Teach about Homosexuality?* Keven DeYoung says:

> In Jesus's mind, to answer the divorce question necessitates a right understanding of marriage, and to get at the nature of marriage one must go back to the beginning, where we see God instituting marriage as the lifelong union of a man and a woman.[8]

DeYoung further says:

> Moreover, monogamy makes sense only within this Genesis understanding of marriage. Apart from the complementarity of the two sexes there is no moral logic which demands that marriage should be restricted to a twosome…. There is no

internal coherence to the notions of monogamy and exclusivity if marriage is something other than the **reunion of two complementary and differentiated sexes**. It's because God made the woman from the man that she is also for the man (1 Cor. 11: 8–9, 11–12). And it's because the two—male and female—are divinely designed complements each for the other that monogamy makes sense and same-sex marriage does not.[9] (Bold added.)

Concerning marriage as being a reflection of Christ and the church, DeYoung says,

> Marriage by its very nature requires complementarity. The mystical union of Christ and the church—each "part" belonging to the other but neither interchangeable—cannot be pictured in marital union without the differentiation of male and female.[10]

Besides creating the perfect pair, God designed a perfect Paradise for Adam and Eve. He gave them language, intelligence, emotion, volition, purpose, meaningful work, and a soul to enjoy each other and Himself. In His wisdom He made such physical union pleasurable as well as purposeful, so that a man and a woman would enjoy their physical union as well as their mutual love, care, and companionship. Everything God created was good; every detail was perfect. Everything Adam and Eve were created to do also brought pleasure. **They needed food to survive, so God made food flavorsome. They were to procreate, so God made their sexual intercourse pleasurable.** God created humans for a love relationship with Himself and with each other. In love He revealed Himself to them and communicated with them.

Life in the Garden was pleasurable, not burdensome. Adam and Eve were able to communicate with each other and with God Himself. God gave them an abundance of trees in the garden with fruit to eat and enjoy. However, right in the midst of such a lavish quantity, quality, and variety of delicious food stood one tree bearing fruit that God forbade them to eat. God gave them only one restriction:

> And the Lord God commanded the man, saying, Of every tree of the garden thou mayest freely eat: But of the tree of the knowledge of good and evil, thou shalt not eat of it: for in the day that thou eatest thereof thou shalt surely die. (Gen. 2:16-17.)

God had clearly communicated His one instruction, which was for their good and which also would give them an opportunity to exercise their God-given volition and their love for and trust in their Creator.

The Beginning of Man's Rebellion Against God

Adam and Eve had everything except permission to eat from "the tree of the knowledge of good and evil." They experienced God's gracious love and kindness as He abundantly provided everything for them. They experienced the wonder of each other, newly created. They had everything they needed to be satisfied—until the tempter attracted Eve's attention.

> Now the serpent was more subtil than any beast of the field which the LORD God had made. And

he said unto the woman, Yea, hath God said, Ye shall not eat of every tree of the garden? And the woman said unto the serpent, We may eat of the fruit of the trees of the garden: But of the fruit of the tree which is in the midst of the garden, God hath said, Ye shall not eat of it, neither shall ye touch it, lest ye die. And the serpent said unto the woman, Ye shall not surely die: For God doth know that in the day ye eat thereof, then your eyes shall be opened, and ye shall be as gods, knowing good and evil. And when the woman saw that the tree was good for food, and that it was pleasant to the eyes, and a tree to be desired to make one wise, she took of the fruit thereof, and did eat, and gave also unto her husband with her; and he did eat. (Gen. 3:1-6.)

The Genesis account reveals how temptation works today. **Temptation begins first by questioning what God has said and then by substituting what God has said is right and good with a personal, man-centered view of what is right and good, based on one's feelings and desires that are in conflict with God's purposes and design.** When human beings forget that "the LORD he is God: it is he that hath made us, and not we ourselves" (Ps. 100:3) and form their own ideas of what is right and good, they are vulnerable to all kinds of temptations and develop a worldview that places humanity (themselves) at the center.

There are now two overall worldviews: the first is God-centered in which God's Word reveals what is right and good; the second is man-centered in its various forms of selfism, humanism, idolatry, and Satan-inspired spirituality. A person's worldview will affect every thought and action directly or indirectly. Here in this book we show forth a biblical, God-centered view regarding: (1) God's great love for mankind as revealed both in creation and redemption; (2) God's wrath against sin; (3) and God's amazing remedy for those who deserve His wrath. Therefore, throughout this book, even while we point out the biblical truth regarding sexual sin, we desire to show forth the marvelous grace of God wherein Christ bore the wrath of God against sin in His body on the cross, so that those who believe the Gospel will be transformed.

The first temptation and the subsequent fall into sin presented a man-centered worldview and its progression can be boiled down to: (1) questioning God's Word, (2) denying God's Word, (3) questioning God's motive, (4) sowing seeds of dissatisfaction, (5) stimulating desire for forbidden fruit, and (6) enticing the person into believing a lie. Satan has been a liar and deceiver from the beginning and continues his crafty lies, gilded with a deceptive touch of truth. A murderer from the beginning, the serpent Satan continues to lie, deceive, and destroy.

Eve was not tainted with sin prior to listening to the serpent. She could have resisted the devil by turning to God and submitting to Him. In his *Notes on the Pentateuch*, C. H. Mackintosh shows how Satan can entice with just four words, "Yea, hath God said":

> This was Satan's crafty inquiry, and had the Word of God been dwelling richly in Eve's heart, her answer might have been direct, simple and conclusive…. To admit the question, "Hath God said?" when I know God has spoken, is posi-

tive infidelity; and the very fact of admitting it, proves my incapacity to meet it. Hence, in Eve's case, the form of her reply evidenced the fact that she had admitted to her heart the serpent's crafty inquiry. Instead of adhering strictly to the exact words of God, she, in her reply, actually adds thereto…. Eve would never have stood by to hear God contradicted if she had not previously fallen into looseness and indifferene as to His Word…. She suffered God to be contradicted by a creature, simply because His Word had lost its proper authority over her heart, her conscience and her understanding.[11]

Eve questioned God's Word and was deceived. Adam, however, knew better and could have sought God to extend mercy to Eve. Yet, since Eve did not die on the spot, he readily received the fruit from the "tree of the knowledge of good and evil." But, as soon as Adam ate, things were different and went downhill from that moment until today: "And the eyes of them both were opened, and they knew that they were naked; and they sewed fig leaves together, and made themselves aprons" (Gen. 3:7). Once pleasurable, their sexuality bore a foreboding face. Their pure openness with one another—their pure relationship of knowing and being known—was tainted. They were no longer free to be and to do, but instead were bound to cover and hide.

Adam and Eve lost much of the pleasure of being together as one, as they had flawlessly experienced mutual love and purely reunited organically through God-designed sex. They lost their Paradise and their purity. Although physical death would not culminate for a number of years, they would eventually die. Their life would be marked by pain and hardship. God cast them out of the Garden, but even that was for their benefit, because if they had eaten from the tree of life after partaking of the tree of the knowledge of good and evil, their misery would have had no end. Living eternally unfulfilled lives with much misery and conflict would be like living in hell.

Ever since that dreadful day, sexuality has been distorted in numerous ways. On one hand, some consider sex itself as unclean and not to be mentioned. Some heterosexual married couples have even felt embarrassed about their spouse seeing them naked and/or are unable to fully enjoy that which God said is good—that which God purposed for bearing children and bringing pleasure. On the other hand, the purity of the original design for sexuality has been sexually corrupted. Various societies throughout history have gloried in orgies of all kinds outside the union of one man and one woman. **Nevertheless the perfect pattern remains and the biblical standard of human sexuality continues to be the sexual union of one man and one woman within the confines of marriage and according to sexual behavior designed by God for mutual love and procreation.** A couple cannot become one organically through oral or anal sex. Neither can two of the same sex become one.

God's Natural Law

Every physical thing in God's creation follows physical laws that can be investigated and depended on. However, there are certain matters in which the truth is assumed to be self-evident. We call these truths "axioms." Synonyms are "accepted truth" and "general truth." An example from geometry would be: "A straight line is the shortest distance between two points." No proof is needed. It is self-evident.

Natural law is God's revelation of Himself as Creator both through physical law and moral law written in the conscience (Rom. 1:19-21; 2:14-15). God endowed humans with a conscience, an inborn sense of right and wrong, along with the ability to think, understand, and reason. An application of "Natural Law" is "use things according to their purpose."[12] Regarding the natural law, William Blackstone, a famous jurist of the 18th century, said:

> Man, considered as a creature, must necessarily be subject to the laws of his creator, for he is an entirely dependent being....And consequently as man depends absolutely upon his maker for every thing, it is necessary that he should in all points conform to his maker's will. This will of his maker is called the law of nature.[13]

The moral law goes beyond the physical to a right and wrong way each aspect of creation is to operate or be used. In other words, "use things according to their purpose."

God created each organ of the body for a purpose. The anus is the end of the gastrointestinal tract, out of which fecal matter is expelled. Fecal matter is a waste product of the body; it carries harmful microbes that can carry disease. **Obviously, according to natural law, God did not create the mouth or anus as an organ of sexual intercourse. It is unnatural to put a repro-**

ductive organ into another person's mouth or anus. Such acts go against God's design. Likewise, God did not create the vagina or clitoris for the tongue or the tongue for the vagina or clitoris. These sexual deviations were created by those who desired sexual pleasure with a person of the same sex, because two persons of the same sex cannot come together according to God's design.

The manner of sexual intercourse, physically designed by God for the possibility for procreation and pleasurable intimacy, matches the sexual organs of the man and the woman. **God's original plan was that a man and woman would copulate through coitus: the insertion of the man's penis into the woman's vagina so that the semen would penetrate the ovum for the opportunity to bring forth new life.** The semen, which contains the seeds of new life, was not created for oral consumption as in oral sex or for anal inclusion. Likewise, other misapplications of other body parts for the purpose of sexual pleasure are destructive deviations from God's design. Such crude corruptions are not sanitized by the "marriage bed"; they are foul forms of uncleanness and rebellion against God's pattern and purpose. God designed coital intercourse for giving life as well as intimate pleasure; perversions of His pattern lead in the opposite direction.

The Marriage Bed

The Letter to the Hebrews says: "Marriage is honourable in all, and the bed undefiled but whoremongers and adulterers God will judge" (Hebrews 13:4). Honourable would be God-pleasing and undefiled would mean that it has not been contaminated by uncleanness or fornication. The Greek word for "bed" in reference to the marriage relationship is "koite," [14] from which the English word "coitus" comes by way of the Latin word "coitus."[15] The Greek word was used as a euphemism for sexual intercourse, but the Latin word "coitus" is defined directly as "a meeting together; sexual union," which would have thus been coital sex. In the context of creation, Hebrews 13:4 speaks of the physical union of husband and wife through coital sexual intercourse.

After the sexual revolution of the 1960s (see Chapter 3), an increasing number of Christians have been expanding the meaning of the verse to include all sexual activity within marriage, no matter how unbiblical or unclean it might be. **Prior to the sexual revolution, Christians understood the biblical standard for marriage to be a committed relationship between one man and one woman uniting as one according to God's original design: coitus.** All other sexual relationships and behaviors were recognized to be sinful, including all homosexual sexual behaviors, such as oral and anal sex.

Primary departures from God's design for sexual activity occur outside the marriage bond of one man and one woman. Such sexual activities come under the designation "fornication," which includes adultery, pornography, prostitution, inordinate desire or lust, rape, molestation, homosexual sexual practices, and beastiality. The word "fornication" is translated from the Greek word *porneia*. According to *The Evangelical Dictionary of Theology*, the word "fornication" has a broader meaning: "In its widest sense *porneia* denotes immorality in general, or every kind of sexual transgression."[16] Thus it includes anything unlawful, and in this case, the natural law would apply. "Uncleanness" would include fornication and everything else that distorts or supplants God's original design for sex.

Oral and anal sex definitely occur under the designation "uncleanness," because they are unclean. As we describe in Chapter 7, these unclean practices can lead to damage and disease. Such unclean activities should never occur within the marital union of one man and one woman. Such inordinate sexual practices are serious violations of God's design, His Word, and natural law. Every one of them moves in the direction of destruction rather than life. We appeal to Christians to think biblically about their sexual practices and to correct any errant sexual practices that deviate from God's design.

God's Love for His Creation

Just as in the beginning, God's laws originated in His love for those He created in His image. Though Adam and Eve were cast from the Garden because of their rebellious disobedience to God's one-rule restriction, God's love for humans continues on—all the way to the cross of Christ, wherein He died in the place of sinners to make them right before God (justified) and to give them new life by which to live by His life and grow into the image of Christ by grace through faith. Therefore, before we proceed to present the biblical view of same-sex practices and other forms of rebellion against God's design of sexuality and God's laws regarding sexual practices, we want to emphasize that God is good. He is not withholding that which is ultimately good for His creation.

God designed men and women perfectly for one another with their corresponding sexual organs uniting them as one flesh to fulfill His plan for mankind. However, after the Fall, mankind devolved through the accumulation of sin and its effect on the entire human race. The Bible clearly states: "Wherefore, as by one man sin entered into the world, and death by sin; and so death passed upon all men, for that all have sinned" (Rom. 5:12). Thus, through generations of sin, both inherited and perpetrated, the original gift of sexual union plunged from perfection to perversion. Because God is holy and just, sin must be punished; yet, because God is love, He paid the eternal penalty for all who believe, receive new life, and follow Him.

Prior to warning us about God's wrath against ever-increasing sinfulness in the first chapter of Romans, Paul extols the power of God in the Gospel, which saves those who hear and respond by grace through faith. Paul emphasizes the righteousness of God as revealed in the Gospel, whereby both His great mercy and perfect justice were satisfied, and by which Christians live by faith:

> For I am not ashamed of the gospel of Christ: for it is the power of God unto salvation to every one that believeth; to the Jew first, and also to the Greek. For therein is the righteousness of God revealed from faith to faith: as it is written, the just shall live by faith. (Romans 1:16-17.)

Therefore, God's gift of salvation is to everyone who believes the Gospel and thereby receives forgiveness, justification, and new life in Christ Jesus. God's righteousness shows forth in the Gospel and believers are to live by faith in God's righteousness rather than in their own righteousness. By God's merciful grace they live by faith in God and His Word instead of trying to earn His acceptance. This glorious truth precedes the verses that reveal the devastating consequences of rejecting God and replacing Him with any man-made god (idol) or man-centered religion (idolatry).

Christ came to redeem His creation and, with that redemption, believers are given new life whereby they are enabled by the Holy Spirit to glorify God. They thus have the ability to glorify Him in their bodies as they unite in marriage, in purity and holiness, according to His original sexual design, with their corresponding sexual organs. **Our plea is to Christian couples—that they reflect His unadulterated design for sexual union in both faithfulness and form.**

2

The Biblical View of Homosexuality

Why are we focusing on homosexual sin? We do so because numerous Christians are becoming more accepting of sexual practices **clearly forbidden by Scripture**. They are being aggressively confronted by a satanic worldview that is dramatically different from that which is clearly shown in Scripture regarding sexual practices. In addition, many Christians have loved ones who are living in homosexual relationships and find it difficult to know how to express their love without compromising their beliefs. They are being confronted with the temptation to adjust their faith to accommodate the conflict between God's Word and the opposing pressures around them.

We are living in an era in which much that is evil is called "good" and good "evil": "Woe unto them that call evil good, and good evil; that put darkness for light, and light for darkness; that put bitter for sweet, and sweet for bitter!" (Isaiah 5:20). Expressions of true love for lost sinners are now labeled "hate," and anyone who opposes the homosexual agenda is labeled "homophobic." Homosexuals have worked hard to educate the public into believing that homosexual practices are normal, natural, and good. After all, what can be wrong with one person loving another person? They have succeeded in convincing many heterosexuals that what men do with men sexually and what women do with women sexually might enhance heterosexual pleasure as well. Moreover, they contend that much of what they do is no different from what many heterosexuals are actually doing already. And if everyone is doing it, what can be wrong?

Many Christians are confused. They know that God is a God of love and compassion; yet His wrath is against same-sex practices, which violate His sexual design for mankind. Some may have a lopsided view of God's love and separate it from what the Bible says about sexual relationships between persons. **Same-sex practices are sinful according to the Bible and will bring forth the just wrath of God unless there is repentance**. Scripture is clear on this issue, not only in the Old Testament, but also in the New Testament, as seen in Romans One and elsewhere. **The only acceptable sexual relationship according to God's creation is between one man and one woman within the covenant of marriage and according to His design, which is coital intercourse.**

The following Scriptures having to do with fornication and lasciviousness are addressed to Christians. Therefore, as we warn about sinful sexual practices, we desire that our words fulfill the responsibility to warn without going beyond the limitations of Scripture.

> But fornication, and all uncleanness, or covetousness, let it not be once named among you, as

becometh saints.... And have no fellowship with the unfruitful works of darkness, but rather reprove them. For it is a shame even to speak of those things which are done of them in secret. But all things that are reproved are made manifest by the light: for whatsoever doth make manifest is light (Eph. 5:3, 11-13).

One can see from verse 3 that the context is primarily sexual sins, which are central in the "unfruitful works of darkness." In their commentary on these verses, E. K. Simpson and F.F. Bruce speak to the need for shedding light on certain hidden sins when they say: "Not only must believers not lend them countenance or partake of other men's sins by a conspiracy of silence, but when occasion serves, it is theirs to drag them to light." However, they also contend that discretion is necessary because of the admonition: "For it is a shame even to speak of those things which are done of them in secret." Therefore they explain:

> A distinction seems to be drawn between two discrepant classes of transgressions. Some are too foul to be mentioned by sanctified lips. These ranker abominations, like rotting carcasses, ought to be buried out of sight. But iniquities of a less heinous cast, compatible with a conscience not utterly seared, should be rebuked by shedding the light of heaven on their obliquity [immorality].[1]

Because some of the sexual practices of homosexuals and many heterosexuals, including many Christians, "are too foul to be mentioned by sanctified lips," we will speak in detail only about the two most

common sexual practices—oral and anal sex—and will refrain from describing the more egregious sinful activities that go even further beyond the limits of God's design. However, we must add that oral and anal sexual sins are only the tip of the iceberg of gross forms of sin that homosexuals and others have invented to gratify themselves sexually, as many have become those "who being past feeling have given themselves over unto lasciviousness, to work all uncleanness with greediness" (Eph. 4:19).

Prior to describing what happened in Sodom, we provide a few definitions. We repeat the legal dictionary definition of "sodomy": "*Sodomy* refers to anal or oral sex, whether between a man and a woman, two women, or two men."[2] The National Health Services in the United Kingdom defines "oral sex": "Oral sex is when you stimulate your partner's genitals with your mouth, lips or tongue. This could involve sucking or licking their penis (also called fellatio), vagina, vulva or clitoris (cunnilingus)...."[3] According to one definition, "Anal sex or anal intercourse is generally the insertion and thrusting of the erect penis into a person's anus, or anus and rectum for sexual pleasure."[4]

A "homosexual" is "a person who is sexually attracted to people of their own sex."[5] That applies to men who are sexually attracted to men and to women who are sexually attracted to women. The dictionary definition of "activism" is "a doctrine or practice that emphasizes direct vigorous action especially in support of or opposition to one side of a controversial issue."[6] An "activist" is "An especially active, vigorous advocate of a cause."[7] "Revisionism" is: "Advocacy of the revision of an accepted usually long-standing view, theory, or doctrine."[8] **An activist homosexual revisionist is one who is a vigorous advocate for reinterpreting the Bible regarding homosexual sexual practices.**

Activist homosexual revisionists, to which we refer here, are activists who "vigorously advocate" for a change in the traditional biblical view of sodomy and other sinful sexual practices of homosexuals. There is nothing wrong with being a revisionist when revision is based on solid biblical evidence and teachings, but the homosexual revisionists lack these requirements.[9] As we said in the "Introduction": Although we will be presenting what the Bible reveals about homosexuality and homosexual practices, our focus is not to confront the homosexual revised view of Scripture. **We are writing to and for Bible-believing Christians.**

The Genesis Account

Why did we title this book *The Sodomy of Christians: The Biblical View*? What does this have to do with the city of Sodom in the Old Testament? Throughout Scripture the city of Sodom stands for extreme forms of evil and debauchery, particularly **same-gender sexual practices**. Sodom is known for its violent destruction because of its severe sinfulness of widespread activity of men lusting after men and fornicating with them.

Early descriptions of Sodom include a vast web of wickedness and rebellion against God. Genesis 13:13 says, "But the men of Sodom were wicked and sinners before the LORD exceedingly." Later in Genesis, just after God had promised a son to Abraham and Sarah, who would be in the birth-line of carrying the seed of

God's Redeemer, Jesus Christ, God told Abraham about His plans to utterly destroy Sodom: "Because the cry of Sodom and Gomorrah is great, and because their sin is very grievous" (Gen. 18:20). Abraham was concerned for his nephew Lot, who lived in Sodom. Thus, knowing God's mercy and kindness, Abraham asked God:

> Wilt thou also destroy the righteous with the wicked? Peradventure there be fifty righteous within the city: wilt thou also destroy and not spare the place for the fifty righteous that are therein? That be far from thee to do after this manner, to slay the righteous with the wicked: and that the righteous should be as the wicked, that be far from thee: Shall not the Judge of all the earth do right? (Gen. 18:21-25.)

God agreed to spare Sodom if there were fifty righteous and even if there were only ten righteous! God's mercy is great and His kindness is longsuffering. But when evil increases to the point of danger to God's people, He must exercise His wrath. God is love, but His love is a protective love that must oppose that which is evil and harmful to His gracious and glorious plan for humanity. His love and justice call for holy wrath when His goodness is opposed by evil and is destructive to His creation. In his second epistle, Peter reminds believers about God:

> ...turning the cities of Sodom and Gomorrah into ashes condemned them with an overthrow, making them an ensample unto those that after should live ungodly; and delivered just Lot, vexed with the filthy conversation of the wicked: (For that

righteous man dwelling among them, in seeing and hearing, vexed his righteous soul from day to day with their unlawful deeds). (2 Pe 2:6-8.)

The biblical account of the men of the city demanding that Lot's guests come out that they might know them reveals that the sin being exposed was men sexually lusting after men:

> And there came two angels to Sodom at even; and Lot sat in the gate of Sodom: and Lot seeing them rose up to meet them; and he bowed himself with his face toward the ground; And he said, Behold now, my lords, turn in, I pray you, into your servant's house, and tarry all night, and wash your feet, and ye shall rise up early, and go on your ways. And they said, Nay; but we will abide in the street all night. And he pressed upon them greatly; and they turned in unto him, and entered into his house; and he made them a feast, and did bake unleavened bread, and they did eat. But before they lay down, the men of the city, even the men of Sodom, compassed the house round, both old and young, all the people from every quarter: And they called unto Lot, and said unto him, Where are the men which came in to thee this night? bring them out unto us, that we may know them. (Gen. 19:1-5.)

The expression translated "that we may know them" means knowing someone sexually, and in this context it means engaging in sodomy (oral and anal sex) and probably other sinful sexual acts.

Making matters more transparent, Lot says, "I pray you, brethren, do not so wickedly" (Gen. 19:7), and then says:

> Behold now, I have two daughters which have not known man; let me, I pray you, bring them out unto you, and do ye to them as is good in your eyes: only unto these men do nothing; for therefore came they under the shadow of my roof. (Gen. 19:8.)

Allen Ross, in *The Bible Knowledge Commentary*, speaks of Lot's egregious error and the clarity of the passage revealing the homosexual nature of the intended sin:

> They wanted to **have sex with** (lit., "to know," i.e., sexually) Lot's visitors. They wanted homosexual relations with these two who they thought were men. As angels, they apparently were handsome. The men's vileness was matched, surprisingly, by Lot's hypocrisy, for he was willing to give them his virgin **daughters** (19:8). To protect one's guests was part of hospitality, but this was going too far![10] (Emphasis in original.)

Kurt Strassner, in his book *Opening Up Genesis*, presents a compelling view of Lot, which is similar to what Christians are facing.

> Lot was a man confused—torn between his upbringing in the faith and his enjoyment of the world. So confused, in fact, that when the men of the city were at the door, prepared to gang-rape his guests [sodomize them], he offered them his daughters instead (19:4–8). Do you see the tor-

ment in his soul? He was desperate to protect his guests, as the LORD would want. But he was also desperate to make peace with the sinful culture in which he lived. So desperate, in fact, that he was willing to sell his daughters in the process.[11]

Lot's offer of his two virgin daughters is atrocious, but perhaps he knew the men would not be interested. Their refusal of Lot's offer clearly reveals their homosexual lust. Rather than appeasing them, Lot's offer enrages them.

> And they said, Stand back. And they said again, This one fellow came in to sojourn, and he will needs be a judge: now will we deal worse with thee, than with them. And they pressed sore upon the man, even Lot, and came near to break the door. (Gen. 19:9.)

At that point the two men (angels) pulled Lot back in and smote the lustful crowd with blindness so that they could not find their way. Next they instructed Lot that he and his family must flee, "For we will destroy this place, because the cry of them is waxen great before the face of the LORD; and the LORD hath sent us to destroy it" (Gen. 19:13). Although numerous forms of sin abounded in Sodom, **the Genesis account clearly indicates that the primary sins involved fornication and "going after strange flesh," which, in the context of Genesis, would be fornication between men.** Later, Jude reveals that "Sodom and Gomorrha, and the cities about them in like manner, giving themselves over to fornication, and going after strange flesh, are set forth for an example, suffering the vengeance of eternal fire" (Jude 7). The combination of the words "fornication" and "strange flesh" refers to male to male, same-gender sexual practices.

In his extensive and well-documented book *As We Sodomize America*, O. R. Adams says:

> The destruction of Sodom and Gomorrah was the only instance in the Bible where people so offended God that he chose to destroy two cities in their entirety. It is equally clear that their primary sins with which God was displeased were "the filthy conversations of the wicked." And that "conversations" as used in that passage meant sexual intercourse, which has been a common meaning of that word until this day. Without question, from these biblical passages the word "sodomy" was developed, as synonymous with homosexuality. And from Bible times until modern times, Sodom and Gomorrah were considered the ultimate of vileness and depravity.[12]

Homosexual acts throughout history are first and foremost a virulent violation of God's sexual design for mankind and "the ultimate of vileness and depravity."

God's Law Regarding Same-Gender Sexual Practices

Although Christians are not "under the law, but under grace" (Rom. 6:14), God's law reveals His standard for what is right and what is wrong and therefore sinful. Thus, the moral law identifies sin and is still applicable for knowing what is displeasing to God. Both the Old Testament laws regarding sexual practices and the

New Testament descriptions of behavior that incur God's judgment need to be known and obeyed. The purpose of the law for New Testament believers is clearly stated in First Timothy 1:8-10:

> But we know that the law is good, if a man use it lawfully; knowing this, that the law is not made for a righteous man, but for the lawless and disobedient, for the ungodly and for sinners, for unholy and profane, for murderers of fathers and murderers of mothers, for manslayers, for whoremongers, for **them that defile themselves with mankind**, for mensteelers, for liars, for perjured persons, and if there be any other thing that is contrary to sound doctrine. (Bold added.)

The act of defiling oneself with mankind is sodom .[13]

Leviticus is clear about God's rules concerning male to male sexual activity. Leviticus 18 begins with God warning the children of Israel not to follow the sinful sexual practices of the Egyptians or the Canaanites. After listing such sexual sins as incest, fornication with other family members, and adultery, Leviticus 18:22 says: "Thou shalt not lie with mankind, as with womankind: it is abomination."

Warren Wiersbe, in his book *Be Holy,* says:

> This section climaxes with prohibitions against homosexuality (18:22) and bestiality (v. 23; see Ex. 22:19; Deut. 27:21), with the warning that these sins are defiling, detestable (NIV), and a perversion (NIV). [14]

In commenting on the consequences of sexual sins described in Leviticus 18:22-30, Wiersbe says:

The picture here isn't a pretty one. Sexual perversions are like disease germs; they make a society and a nation sick. Then the land itself becomes sick and must vomit out its filthy people the way a human body vomits out poison. How tragic that people made in God's image should end up as vomit! Please note that these were *Gentile* nations that were judged—peoples with whom God had not made any covenants, but He still held them accountable for their filthy deeds against nature (Rom. 1:18ff).

If God so dealt with *Gentile* nations, to whom He'd never given His law, how much more will He hold accountable those who claim to know Him and possess His Word? There are dire consequences to sexual sins, and the judgment is greatest where the light has been the brightest. Alas, the nation of Israel disobeyed God, defiled their land, and were vomited out into captivity. Today, there are both secular and religious organizations that openly espouse an immoral lifestyle contrary to God's Word; in God's eyes, they're making society sick. (Italics his.) [15]

Matthew Henry brings his wisdom to Leviticus 18:22-30 in saying:

A law against unnatural lusts, sodomy and bestiality, sins not to be named nor thought of without the utmost abhorrence imaginable, v. 22, 23. Other sins level men with the beasts, but these sink them much lower. That ever there should have been occasion for the making of these laws, and that since they are published they should ever have been broken, is the perpetual reproach and scandal of human nature; and the giving of men up to these vile affections was frequently the punishment of their idolatries; so the apostle shows, Rom. 1:24.[16]

Not only is such same-gender sexual activity sinful, "it is an abomination." In his book *What Does the Bible Really Teach about Homosexuality?* Kevin DeYoung explains when the meaning of the word "abomination" refers specifically to homosexual sexual sin

> Several sins in the Holiness Code of Leviticus are described as abominations, but only this one is singled out by itself as an abomination. The use of to'ebah in Ezekiel [16:50], with reference to Sodom's sin, is an echo of Leviticus 18 and 20. Sodom's sins were many: pride, social injustice, and **pursuing homosexual behavior**.[17] (Bold added.)

Mosaic Law required the death penalty for committing abomination: "If a man also lie with mankind, as he lieth with a woman, both of them have committed an abomination: they shall surely be put to death; their blood shall be upon them" (Lev. 20:13).

Andrew Knowles explains:

> Sexual sins such as adultery, incest, homosexuality and bestiality all carry the death penalty. Such behaviour must be cut like a cancer from the body of God's people. Some of the laws actually speak of being "cut off"—the guilty person being

> expelled or excommunicated, to prevent infecting others.... [18]

Such laws regarding sexual practices were to protect Israel's health and purity. In fact, the very nations they were to drive out and replace were filled with sexual immorality, which was one reason why the Israelites were to drive them out, rather than to mingle with them and intermarry. Knowles says:

> Among the Canaanites, where the Israelites are heading, sex is a free-for-all. There is sex between family members, sex between people of the same sex, and sex between people and animals. Sex is also involved in the worship of pagan gods, which are themselves sexually permissive and perverted."[19]

The New Testament carries the same prohibitions against same-sex sexual practices, but at the same time gives hope through the Gospel. 1 Corinthians says:

> Know ye not that the unrighteous shall not inherit the kingdom of God? Be not deceived: neither fornicators, nor idolaters, nor adulterers, **nor effeminate, nor abusers of themselves with mankind**, nor thieves, nor covetous, nor drunkards, nor revilers, nor extortioners, shall inherit the kingdom of God. And such were some of you: but ye are washed, but ye are sanctified, but ye are justified in the name of the Lord Jesus, and by the Spirit of our God. (1 Cor. 6:9-11, bold added.)

Like-gender sexual practices are included in the above list of those who will "not inherit the kingdom of God." Yet, those who have been saved by Christ and given new life, whereby they have power to overcome such sinful practices, enter into Christ's kingdom by grace through faith.

While Paul uses the description "abusers of themselves with mankind" in 1 Corinthians, he uses a slightly different description in First Timothy in reference to those practicing homosexuality: "them that defile themselves with mankind" (1 Tim. 1:10). The meaning is the same and the prohibition is the same. The fact that homosexual practices are listed among many other serious sins in the Bible does not lessen the seriousness or the eternal consequences. One can see in Paul's description in Romans 1 how like-gender sexual practices mock God and His creation and how at one point God gives people over to their own sinful lusts, which, without His merciful intervention, will lead to eternal damnation.

Romans 1: Degradation into Same-Sex Practices.

Paul's reasoning in his letter to the Romans begins with the fact that God's wrath is not against the innocent, but against those who practice "ungodliness and unrighteousness":

> For the wrath of God is revealed from heaven against all ungodliness and unrighteousness of men, who hold the truth in unrighteousness; Because that which may be known of God is manifest in them; for God hath shewed it unto them. For the invisible things of him from the creation of the world are clearly seen, being understood by the things that are made, even his eternal pow-

er and Godhead; so that they are without excuse: Because that, when they knew God, they glorified him not as God, neither were thankful; but became vain in their imaginations, and their foolish heart was darkened. (Romans 1:18-21.)

God has revealed enough of Himself through all of creation, as well as by creating man in His image, whereby He gave human beings a conscience and a sense of right and wrong. However, people have immersed the truth in sin to the degree that God's Word says that they "hold the truth in unrighteousness." In other words, they are moral beings who know enough to be responsible for their actions and they are without excuse. As later revealed in Romans, "All have sinned" (Rom. 3:23; 5:12).

In contrast to "The just shall live by faith," (Rom. 1:17), those who walk further and further away from God sink more deeply into unrighteousness. The downward spiral of sin begins by not glorifying God as God, not being thankful, making up one's own ideas of how things should be, and forming a worldview alien to what God has clearly said. Then, by rejecting God's way and forming their own way, those who practice "ungodliness and unrighteousness" enter into the darkness of deception: self-deception and being deceived. These would obviously include atheists, agnostics, and followers of religions not based on the Bible. But, in addition, these would **also include professing Christians who live more unto themselves than unto God, who have adjusted their faith to accommodate their sin, and who thereby live more according to a man-made worldview than according to God's Word.**

> Professing themselves to be wise, they became fools, and changed the glory of the uncorruptible God into an image made like to corruptible man, and to birds, and fourfooted beasts, and creeping things. (Rom. 1:22-23.)

Being in darkness, they consider themselves wise, but are acting as fools, exchanging the glory of God for images of man (male and female) and substituting the worship of God with the worship of man (male and female). Images resembling men and women reveal that the first departure into idolatry is a worship of self: worship practiced for personal gain. Not only that: the degradation plunges into worshipping birds, beasts and "creeping things." Instead of God's truth defining their worldview, they have concocted their own with a collection of creatures and concepts contradicting God. Consequently God gives them over to their sinful lusts.

As they went further away from God and His design and His will and rejected the light, God "gave them up" to do whatever their sinful nature desired:

> Wherefore God also gave them up to **uncleanness** through the **lusts of their own hearts**, to **dishonour their own bodies** between themselves: Who changed the truth of God into a lie, and worshipped and served the creature more than the Creator, who is blessed for ever. Amen. (Rom. 1:24-25, bold added.)

The general term "uncleanness" would include all sexual activity outside His design of one man and one woman in a committed relationship uniting organically through coital intercourse. The Bible does not list all of the forms of sexual sin. The word "uncleanness" covers them all. Sodomy (oral and anal sex) is a perverse use of the organs of sex created for procreation and pleasurable intimacy through coitus. Body parts joined in these unnatural ways go against God's design for sexual intimacy.

Perverted, unnatural sex fosters lust for delving more deeply into sexual corruption. That is why so many homosexuals move into more and more dangerous methods of sexual satisfaction. For heterosexuals, oral sex may diminish the pleasure of natural sex (coitus) and lead to a dependency on oral sex for satisfaction until that is no longer enough. Next comes anal sex. **Perversion leads to lust, which, in turn, leads to more perversion, with more individuals, whether homosexual or heterosexual, dishonoring their bodies**.

In *The New Bible Dictionary*, G. J. Wenham says, "Uncleanness is most often associated with sexual sin (e.g., Rom. 1:24; Gal. 5:19; 1 Thes. 4:7), so that impurity is virtually identified with misuse of sex."[20] Regarding uncleanness, John Gill, in his commentary, says that "all uncleanness takes in adultery, incest, sodomy, and every unnatural lust."[21] Matthew Henry says, "*All uncleanness* includes all other sorts of filthy lusts, which were too common among the Gentiles"[22] (italics in original).

Notice that, when they follow the "lusts of their own hearts," they "dishonor their own bodies between themselves." They do injustice to themselves: "Every sin that a man doeth is without the body; but he that committeth fornication sinneth against his own body" (1 Cor. 6:18). As we shall see later, individuals can damage themselves and each other in numerous ways through sexual sin.

However, the worst punishment is when God lets people go their own way and thereby gives sinners up to their own lusts, because the degradation sinks further down and away from God.

> For this cause God gave them up unto vile affections: for even their women did change the natural use into that which is against nature: And likewise also the men, leaving the natural use of the woman, burned in their lust one toward another; men with men working that which is unseemly, and receiving in themselves that recompense of their error which was meet (Romans 1:26-27).

Unrighteous societies foster sexual unrighteousness. The above passage clearly reveals the biblical standard concerning like-sex sexual practices, which are called "vile affections," "against nature," "unseemly," and "error." What are these "vile affections"? They are inordinate forms of desire, as indicated from the examples that follow: "for even their women did change the natural use into that which is against nature."

A woman's "natural use" is coital sexual intimacy with her husband, childbearing, and nurturance. Her "natural use" designed by God becomes distorted and goes against "nature" and God when she changes her childbearing and nurturance into child-destroying abortion. In believing the lie that a fetus is not yet a human, mothers opt for abortion. The numbers in the United States have increased daily since abortion was made legal in 1973 by Roe v. Wade. To date in this country, nearly 60 million babies have been murdered in the womb, the very organ God created as a nurturing, protective place.[23]

The woman also violates her natural, God-designed use when she engages sexually with another woman. This is clear from the word "likewise" preceding "also the men, leaving the natural use of the woman, burned in their lust one toward another; men with men working that which is unseemly, and receiving in themselves that recompence of their error which was meet" (Romans 1:27).

In commenting on this section of Romans, William MacDonald says:

> For this same reason **God gave** people **up to** erotic activity with members of their own sex. **Women** became lesbians, practicing unnatural sex and knowing no shame.

> **Men** became sodomites, in total perversion of their natural functions. Turning away from the marriage relationship ordained by God, they **burned** with **lust for** other **men** and practiced homosexuality. But their sin took its toll in their bodies and souls. Disease, guilt, and personality deformities struck at them like the sting of a scorpion. This disproves the notion that anyone can commit this sin and get away with it.

> Homosexuality is being passed off today by some as a sickness and by others as a legitimate alternative lifestyle. Christians must be careful not to accept the world's moral judgments but to be guided by God's word. In the OT, this sin was punishable by death (Lev. 18:29; 20:13), and here in the NT those who practice it are said to be worthy of death (Rom. 1:32). The Bible speaks of

homosexuality as a very serious sin, as evidenced by God's obliteration of Sodom and Gomorrah, where militant "gays" ran riot (Gen. 19:4–25).[24] (Bold in original.)

One cannot read the first chapter of Romans honestly without coming to the conclusion that homosexual practices are sinful and bring forth the wrath of God. Although like-gender sexual practices are not the only sinful activities that call for God's wrath, one must not minimize the sinfulness of same-gender sexual practices by pointing the finger at people who are engaging in other serious sins. All disobedience to God is sinful and, without God's saving grace, results in eternal damnation. However, regarding the nature of sin, while all are serious, same-gender (male to male or female to female) sexual sins violate the creation of man and woman and their God-ordained marriage relationship, which is used in Scripture to represent God's relationship with His people (Eph. 5:22-32).

All sin mocks God, but **homosexual (male with male or female with female) sexual sin defies God's creation of man in His own image: male and female; despoils His gift of intimate relationship in the uniting of male and female into one flesh; and desecrates His redemptive plan for relationship with His children as pictured in the marriage of Christ and His bride, which is comprised of all true believers.**

Same-gender sexual practices are most obvious in societies that are filled with other serious forms of unrighteousness as seen in Romans 1:26-32. Such societies both encourage and support behavior that is in rebellion against God, because they, too, refuse to honor Him as

God. They, too, have erected their own idols and thumbed their noses at God. Even when they know God's judgment of sin, they both sin and take pleasure in the sins of others. Those who approve of the sins of others are operating from a self-centered, satanic worldview.

Romans 1:18-32 shows forth a pattern of events that are followed by pagan societies that set up their own idols and practice all forms of sexual sin. Hebrew scholars contend that homosexual relationships were a primary reason for the Flood. Gail Labovitz, in her article "Same-Sex Marriage," says:

> There are several rabbinic passages which take up, or very likely take up, the subject of same-sex marital unions—always negatively. In each case, homosexual marriage (particularly male homosexual marriage) is rhetorically stigmatized as the practice of non-Jewish (or pre-Israelite) societies, and is presented as an outstanding marker of the depravity of those societies; homosexual marriage is thus clearly associated with the Other [other nations]. The first three of the four rabbinic texts presented here also associate homosexual marriage with bestiality. These texts also employ a rhetoric of fear: **societal recognition of such homosexual relationships will bring upon that society extreme forms of Divine punishment— the destruction of the generation of the Flood, the utter defeat of the Egyptians at the Exodus, the wiping out of native Canaanite peoples in favor of the Israelites.**[25] (Bold added.)

According to archeology, the history of homosexuality, practiced by men with men and women with women, extends back through the centuries. Regarding ancient Egyptians, the first recorded same-sex male homosexual relationship occurred in Egypt around 2400 BC.[26] Vern L. Bullough, in his book *Sexual Variance in Society and History*, says, "All sexual activities, from bestiality to anal intercourse to oral-genital contacts are portrayed in the various tomb pictures, and though the Egyptians might have disapproved some activities more than others, their society seemed to be fairly permissive sexually."[27] **Bullough is a secular humanist, but, in his objective view of the history of homosexuality, he says in reference to Scripture: "Adultery, fornication, homosexuality, and perhaps even masturbation were condemned."[28] He also affirms that 1 Timothy 1:10 and Romans 1:26-27 "quite clearly deal with homosexuality"[29]** (bold added).

In contrast to those homosexuals who revise Scripture to accommodate their sexual preferences and practices, many homosexuals affirm that the Bible teaches against homosexuality—that the orthodox understandings of Scripture about homosexuality are what the Bible says. For example, Louis Crompton, an internationally known scholar who has received many awards and honors during his career and who is himself a homosexual, says that the Bible is indeed speaking negatively about homosexuality. In his book *Homosexuality & Civilization*, Crompton quotes Romans 1:26-27 as an example of the fact that Paul was indeed referring to homosexuality when he says, "…their women did change the natural use into that which is against nature: and likewise also the men, leaving the natural use of the woman, burned in their lust one toward another…." Compton says that Paul is therein referring to lesbians and homosexuals. He then clearly says: "**Nowhere does Paul or any other Jewish writer of this period imply the least acceptance of same-sex relations under any circumstances**" (bold added). [30]

The number of homosexuals who believe that the Bible condemns homosexuality is always surprising to many Christians. Yet, these unbelievers are simply reading what the Bible clearly says about homosexuality and recognizing that it opposes homosexual practices. **It is their way of saying that the Bible does, in fact, teach that homosexuality is sin, which is reason enough for them to reject the Bible all together.**

All Bible believing Christians should recognize that the Bible teaches against all variances from God's sexual design. As J. A. Witmer, says in *The Bible Knowledge Commentary*:

> The only natural sexual relationship the Bible recognizes is a heterosexual one (Gen. 2:21–24; Matt. 19:4–6) within marriage. All homosexual relations constitute sexual **perversion** and are subject to God's judgment. Such lustful and **indecent acts** have within them the seeds of punishment (**due penalty**). [31] (Emphasis in original.)

"Born That Way"?

The New Atlantis: A Journal of Technology & Society published a "Special Report titled "Sexuality and Gender." [32] Dr. Ryan T. Anderson, who is a Senior Research Fellow at the Heritage Foundation, says that the new report "challenges the leading narratives that the media has pushed regarding sexual orientation and gender identity." He continues:

> Co-authored by two of the nation's leading scholars on mental health and sexuality, the 143-page report discusses over 200 peer-reviewed studies in the biological, psychological, and social sciences, painstakingly documenting what scientific research shows *and does not show* about sexuality and gender.

> The major takeaway, as the editor of the journal explains, is that "some of the most frequently heard claims about sexuality and gender are not supported by scientific evidence."[33] (Emphasis in original.)

In the "Executive Summary," under "Part One: Sexual Orientation," the two authors, Dr. Lawrence S. Mayer and Dr. Paul R. McHugh, conclude:

> The understanding of sexual orientation as an innate, biologically fixed property of human beings—the idea that people are "born that way"—is not supported by scientific evidence [34]

This extensive scholarly study obviously contradicts the "born that way" shibboleths of the homosexual activists. We include this supportive research even though the final Word is always the Bible.

"Can't Change"?

"Can't change" is another homosexual activist shibboleth. The idea that choice is involved and change is possible is an anathema to many of them. They want everyone to believe that change is impossible because they are supposedly "born that way." Instead of change they want affirmation and support so that they can follow their sexual desires and practices. They want the public to believe that their sexual choices are fully fixed and normal.

Indeed habits do become fairly fixed and are difficult to change, and particularly habits that change the brain through pleasure. Moreover, **considering the power of sex and lust, change may be extremely difficult, which is why so many believe it is impossible.** Then, those who believe they cannot change and have become confirmed in their faith in "can't change" will be convinced that change is impossible. And, let's face it: many who identify as gay or lesbian **do not want to change**.

But change is possible! "Can't change" is myth based on faith, not fact. Laurie Higgins, in her article "Homosexuals Admit 'Sexual Orientation' Can and Does Change," says that the "Can't change" claims "are patently false."[35] In her article she quotes scholars and professors, all of whom are themselves homosexuals or lesbians. Every one of them affirms the fact that sexuality is fluid rather than fixed. She quotes the following from Camille Paglia, who is a feminist scholar and lesbian: "Sexuality is highly fluid, and reversals are theoretically possible. However, a habit is refractory, once the sensory pathways have been blazed and deepened by repetition."[36]

Jane Ward, who is a lesbian, says:

But the fact that the "born this way" hypothesis has resulted in greater political returns for gay and lesbian people doesn't have anything to do with whether it is true. Maybe, as gay people, we want to get together and *pretend* it is true because it is politically strategic… That would be interesting. But still, it wouldn't make the idea true…. People like to cite "the overwhelming scientific evidence" that sexual orientation is biological in nature. But show me a study that claims to have proven this, and I will show you a flawed research design…. People like to use the failure of "gay conversion" therapies as evidence that homosexuality is innate. **First of all, these conversions do not always fail….the point is that we can and do change.**[37] (Italics in original; bold added.)

Trudy Ring, a writer for *The Advocate*, which is a homosexual magazine," says:

For years, much of the case for LGBT rights has been based on the argument that sexual orientation is fixed and immutable—baby we were born this way, and it's wrong to discriminate against us for something we didn't choose.

But an increasing body of social science research posits that a sizable number of people experience some degree of fluidity in their sexual and romantic attractions: being drawn to the same gender at one point in their life, the opposite gender at another.[38]

Of course, the longer a person has participated in a pleasurable activity on a regular basis, the more ingrained the desire becomes and a habit develops and solidifies. Research on gambling addiction reveals that one does not have to smoke or take opiates to become addicted. The pleasure centers in the brain are engaged during sex and, when certain forms of sexual practice prevail, such as oral or anal sex, the desire increases and turns to lust. The more one fantasizes or does it, the more one desires it. Sexual activities affect the brain and can even alter it. **Same-sex sexual activities can dramatically change the brain, particularly when such activities are fantasized and practiced on a regular basis over time and even more so when started at a vulnerable age, such as childhood or adolescence.** Homosexual identity and desire can **feel** firmly fixed—immutable. However, although new habits of sexual desire and restraint may be difficult to change, they are possible!

New Identity in Christ

We do not expect gays, lesbians, or bisexuals to change through their own efforts, although many have. We believe that, instead of changing from gay, lesbian, or bisexual to heterosexual, individuals can be saved and given a new identity in Christ. Homosexuality is actually a symptom of the unredeemed old nature, also called the flesh or the old man. But there is hope in Christ! Because of God's great love for His creation, He has provided forgiveness and new life. Christ came to reveal God and to die in the place of sinners. Thus, when a person trusts in Christ's death on the cross—that Christ died in his/her place thereby taking the just punishment of sin—that person receives new life, which is the very life of Christ living within by means of the Holy Spirit.

The believer is so deeply related to Christ that he/she has a **new identity in Christ!** The apostle Paul says: "Therefore if any man be in Christ, he is a new creature: old things are passed away; behold, all things are become new" (2 Cor. 5:17). This **new life** does not sin (1 John 3:9). However, believers still carry around their old nature, referred to as the flesh. Thus, even after a person receives this new life, the flesh must be conquered by means of the Holy Spirit. As one reads the New Testament, one sees that, although there is a warfare between the flesh (old nature) and the spirit (new nature), the Holy Spirit within the believer gives power to overcome and to thereby walk according to the Spirit (Gal. 5:16-25).

There are many testimonies of conversions from homosexual sinfulness to salvation in Christ by former gays and lesbians who have died to self and who give witness to the biblical faith that condemns their former life style. One excellent example of a former lesbian is Rosario Butterfield. In an article titled "Love Your Neighbor Enough to Speak Truth," Butterfield says

> To be clear, I was not converted out of homosexuality. I was converted out of unbelief. I didn't swap out a lifestyle. I died to a life I loved. Conversion to Christ made me face the question squarely: did my lesbianism *reflect* who I am (which is what I believed in 1999), or did my lesbianism *distort* who I am through the fall of Adam? I learned through conversion that when something feels right and good and real and necessary—but stands against God's Word—this

reveals the particular way Adam's sin marks my life. Our sin natures deceive us. Sin's deception isn't just "out there"; it's also deep in the caverns of our hearts.

How I feel does not tell me who I am. Only God can tell me who I am, because he made me and takes care of me. He tells me that we are all born as male and female image bearers with souls that will last forever and gendered bodies that will either suffer eternally in hell or be glorified in the New Jerusalem. Genesis 1:27 tells me that there are ethical consequences and boundaries to being born male and female. When I say this previous sentence on college campuses—even ones that claim to be Christian—the student protestors come out in the dozens. I'm told that declaring the ethical responsibilities of being born male and female is now hate speech.[39] (Italics in original.)

In her book titled *The Secret Thoughts of an Unlikely Convert*, Butterfield reflect

As I reread my life, I realized that my sexual sin was rooted not only in pride but also in a false understanding about gender. I came to the understanding that I could not possibly be a godly woman if I didn't even know how to be a woman.[40]

How gracious of our Creator to inspire Paul to put the judgment of sin at the beginning of Romans to bring us all to our knees and then for most of the following chapters in Romans to show forth the glorious answer to all sin and all sinners. "For all have sinned, and come short of the glory of God," and "the wages of sin is death; but the gift of God is eternal life through Jesus Christ our Lord" (Romans 3:23; 6:23). Salvation is available to all who believe the Gospel and receive new life in Christ. **Therefore, Christians who are involved in sexual sin, such as oral and/or anal sex, need to stop, repent, and be conformed to the life of Christ in them.**

3

The Sexual Revolution

The Sexual Revolution of the 1960s through the 1980s dramatically decimated much of the traditional moral foundation of the United States. As external standards of behavior lost their influence, all forms of sexual restraint were called into question and sexual liberation gained ground and accelerated rapidly. Clear rules about fornication being sinful were cast aside and replaced with an ever-increasing acceptance of sex outside of marriage, premarital sex, abortion on demand, homosexuality, pornography, and alternative sexual activities far outside God's design for sexual union. Every deviation from God's design that demanded acceptance, even beyond tolerance, that emerged through this Sexual Revolution has serious consequences and should be shunned by all Christians.

In this book our focus is primarily on Christians as they are living in a society that has not only accepted, but embraced homosexuality with its sexual orientation and numerous sexual practices. **Our concern is that many**

Christians have gone so far in accepting the culture around them that they themselves are now involved in the culture's sexual uncleanness by engaging in at least two homosexual sexual practices: oral and anal sex. How did such changes come about?

During the past fifty-plus years we have seen a rising fulfillme t of Bible prophecy having to do with human nature. Under the guise of science, various branches of anthropology, psychology, and sociology took root and choked out the biblical definition of humanity. The very kind of "science falsely so-called" warned about in Scripture (1 Tim. 6:20) proclaimed that humans evolved from primates and are born with a clean slate (innately good) but corrupted (read "wounded") by circumstances, society, and particularly parents.

Influence of Affluenc

The sexual revolution of the 60s through the 80s could not have occurred during the ten-year period of the depression, which began in 1929. One of the most important ingredients in the sexual revolution is affluence. With increasing affluence, individuals focused more on self-fulfillment and personal satisfaction. The prevailing idea was that, if each person is fulfilled and satisfied, society's ills would be healed. However, rather than that hoped-for conclusion, what we have seen is indeed the fulfillment of 2 Tim. 3:1-5:

> This know also, that in the last days perilous times shall come. For men shall be lovers of their own selves, covetous, boasters, proud, blasphemers, disobedient to parents, unthankful, unholy, without natural affection, trucebreakers, false ac-

cusers, incontinent, fierce, despisers of those that are good, traitors, heady, highminded, lovers of pleasures more than lovers of God; having a form of godliness, but denying the power thereof: from such turn away.

The ever expanding fulfilment of 2 Tim. 3:1-5 was the seed-bed of the twentieth-century sexual revolution. Increasing affluence fueled the influences described in this chapter that gradually turned America from a God honoring country towards a self-honoring nation.

Influence of Secula Humanism

Secular humanists in anthropology, psychology, and sociology worked assiduously for a seemingly more enlightened, emancipated selfhood than ever before existed in America. In her book *Road to Malpsychia*, Joyce Milton notes:

> By the 1960s the stage was set for a radically simplified view of human nature, influenced by existentialism but with a unique American spin. To maximize one's potential, one had to throw off the distorting influences of society and discover and nurture one's innate good self.[1]

Humanistic psychology paved the way for a new concept of the self that needed to be freed from the restraints of "repressive social institutions and moral codes" so that people would be "free to develop their inborn goodness" and "build a society without hypocrisy, prejudice or exploitation."[2] Of course, the church was viewed as a "repressive social institution" with "moral codes" rather than as Christ's body of believers who are truly free in

Him—free from the condemnation of the law and free from the domination of sin. Erroneous, external, Satan-inspired views of Christianity have so overtaken our society that the church is seen as the enemy to personal fulfilment and freedom, when, in fact, this country has become more and more enslaved to sin with its many forms of sexual uncleanness and fornication.

But even before the development of humanistic psychology, the tares had already been sown. Sigmund Freud (1856-1939), considered the father of the psychotherapy movement, believed that morality, particularly sexual morality, was at the root of psychological disorders. He felt that free fornication would be great preventive medicine and psychoprophylactic for the mind. In fact, he believed in a strong, direct relationship between a person's sex life and mental-emotional disorders. He said that "factors arising in sexual life represent the nearest and practically the most momentous causes of every single case of nervous illness."[3]

Freud's only objections to free fornication were the possibilities of venereal disease and pregnancy.[4] Little did he anticipate our present permissive society, which has achieved his great therapeutic ideal of free fornication. Little did he realize that the sexual revolution that followed his conjectures would not only cause more mental-emotional-behavioral disorders, but rip right into the fabric of society. Indeed Freud's influence is such that E.M. Thornton in *The Freudian Fallacy* states:

> Probably no single individual has had a more profound effect on twentieth-century thought than Sigmund Freud. His works have influenced psychiatry, anthropology, social work, penology,

and education and provided a seemingly limitless source of material for novelists and dramatists. Freud has created a "whole new climate of opinion"; for better or worse he has changed the face of society.[5]

Abraham Maslow (1908-1970) followed many of Freud's ideas regarding sexual freedom and belief in a powerful unconscious that motivates behavior. Maslow, considered by many to be one of the founders of humanistic psychology, contended that people are innately good and possess "innate instincts" within themselves to enable them to find values within the self rather than looking to an outside source, such as the Bible.[6] Maslow thus fostered moral relativism, which is similar to and just a step beyond cultural relativism, which is "the idea that a person's beliefs, values, and practices should be understood based on that person's own culture, rather than judged against the criteria of another."[7] In other words, there are no absolutes!

Cultural relativism was originally conceived by Franz Boas (1858-1942), a highly influential anthropologist at Columbia University, where anthropology was studied from a Darwinian evolutionary perspective. Milton explains, "Central to the evolutionist way of thinking was the belief that civilization was progressing toward ever more humane forms of social organization." However, she adds, "Like so much social science theory, it was a thick stew concocted out of meager scraps of fact and large helpings of dubious supposition."[8]

Margaret Mead (1901-1978) and Ruth Benedict (1887-1948) studied under Boas and popularized many of his teachings on cultural relativism.[9] Mead became

a well-known anthropologist through her misguided research, which was later discovered to be mistaken. She
came away from her time on the island of Samoa with the
notion that sexual freedom was a beneficial part of their
culture, because she believed what the island native girls
said about their sex life in response to her questions. She
did not realize, nor did anybody else until many years
later, that these girls were fooling her.[10] Mead's falla-
cious work contributed greatly to the sexual revolution,
providing more "science falsely so-called" to justify all
forms of sexual uncleanness and fornication. She herself
practiced fornication in her affairs with both men and
women.[11]

Benedict called for "redefining normality in a single generation," and, although that seemed a remote
possibility, "her friend and sometime student Abraham
Maslow would lay the groundwork for a new theory of
personality that would do just that."[12] Milton reports that
Maslow adopted Benedict as "his model of the 'good human being,'"[13] even though she saw herself as a deviant,
having suffered much mental torment with depression,
uncontrolled rages and "suicidal impulses" throughout
much of her life. Benedict's answer to life was redefining
normality in order to have her own way in whatever she
pursued, which, like Mead, included sexual relationships
with both men and women.[14] In fact, she justified homosexual practice along with sadism in her paper titled
"Anthropology and the Abnormal," in which she blamed
much abnormal behavior on the restraints of society on
homosexuals and others who do not conform to the traditional norms.[15]

In spite of or because of all this, Maslow deemed Benedict "one of those rare human beings who had managed to become more 'fully human' than the rest of us."[16] Thus Maslow created his humanistic personality theory with its hierarchy of needs and envisioned a new utopia, which he called "Eupsychia": "an ideal community of one thousand psychologically healthy people," which would be "anarchistic" since no one would "need to impose their opinions, religious beliefs, or personal tastes on others."[17] Maslow's dream for a Utopia inhabited with self-actualized persons of high self-esteem was realized in the Haight-Ashbury district of San Francisco, as the flower children of the sixties took his theories to heart and lived a life of free love and self-gratification [18] Maslow did not teach self-indulgence, but that is the outcome of any system which emphasizes the self, presupposes the goodness of the human, and claims that people will develop their highest potential if so-called needs are met.

Egoism and Self-Esteem

Two other contributors to throwing off society's restraints on personal and sexual freedom were acclaimed novelist and philosopher Ayn Rand (1905-1982) and one of her devotees, self-esteem psychologist Nathanial Branden (1930-2014). Rand's highly popular novels and influential philosophy of Objectivism were highly egocentric. She contended that, through exercising reason, the ego determines reality as it integrates information gleaned through the five senses. She declared

The Objectivist ethics holds that the actor must always be the beneficiary of his action and that man must act for his own *rational* self-interest....

Just as man cannot survive by any random means, but must discover and practice the principles which his survival requires, so man's self-interest cannot be determined by blind desires or random whims, but must be discovered and achieved by the guidance of rational principles. This is why the Objectivist ethics is a morality of *rational* self-interest—or of *rational selfishness*.

Since selfishness is "concern with one's own interests," the Objectivist ethics uses that concept in its exact and purest sense. It is not a concept that one can surrender to man's enemies, nor to the unthinking misconceptions, distortions, prejudices and fears of the ignorant and the irrational. The attack on "selfishness" is an attack on man's self-esteem; to surrender one, is to surrender the other.[19] (Emphasis in original.)

Thus for Rand, self is the arbiter of reality and values. With the centrality of the ego, Rand's philosophy gave her the freedom to have a long-term sexual relationship with Branden. Because Rand's husband and Branden's wife were among Rand's many admiring followers, they did not interfere and continued to remain officially married. However, years later, when Branden engaged in a sexual relationship with another woman, Rand expelled him from his position of training others in her philosophy at her Nathaniel Branden Institute, which was then dissolved.

Interestingly, though Rand's philosophy promoted independent thinking, those under her tutelage were encouraged to think like her to the point that Branden later apologized to former students of Objectivism for "perpetuating the Ayn Rand mystique" and for "contributing to that dreadful atmosphere of intellectual repressiveness that pervades the Objectivist movement."[20] After leaving Rand's Objectivism movement, Branden became known for his own promotion of self-esteem through such books as *The Psychology of Self-Esteem*[21] and *Honoring the Self: Self-Esteem and Personal Transformation.*[22]

The self-esteem movement fueled the sexual revolution. Self must be satisfied and therefore one must not be constrained sexually by societal constraints. The fruit of the self-esteem movement can be seen throughout society. Daniel Yankelovitch reveals in his book entitled *New Rules: Searching for Self-Fulfillment in a World Turned Upside Down*: "In their extreme form, the new rules simply turn the old ones on their head, and in place of the old self-denial ethic we find people who refuse to deny *anything* to themselves" (emphasis in original).[23] And, of course "anything" includes sexual freedom. Today America has come to a place lacking the restraint of self-denial and the earlier restraints of society, thereby leaving the possibilities of sexual activities wide open.

From Sexual Freedom to Entitlement to Victimhood

Along with Maslow's dream of a Utopia comprised of self-actualized persons and Ayn Rand's philosophy setting forth a new morality of pursuing one's own happiness came a Yale law professor, Charles Reich (born

1928). Reich championed the counterculture of the 1960s with the idea that society's institutions had failed and that individuals needed to be free from the constraints of society. He further contended that, to be truly free, people had to recognize their own victimhood. In his book *The Greening of America*, Reich argues that violence occurs when there is "any assault upon, or violation of the personality." By this he means anything that goes against a person's wishes or comfort. These are the examples he gives: "Compulsory gym [class] to one embarrassed or afraid is a form of violence." "The requirement that a student must get a pass to walk in the hallway is a violence." "Compulsory attendance in the classroom, compulsory studying in the study hall, is a form of violence." He concludes by saying that "the amount of violence in high school is staggering."[24]

Reich himself was gay and became active in the early days of the homosexual activist movement. Here seeds of victimization were planted as a component of the sexual revolution along with demands of entitlement. Those fornicating with like-sex partners play the victim role, require a new form of justice, and justify vengeance as seen in the ensuing law suits against those who oppose their sexual agenda.

Alfred Kinsey's Perverted and Pernicious Influenc

In addition to what are called the "soft sciences" of anthropology, psychology, and sociology came what is regarded as a "hard science," one that can usually be investigated because one is dealing with physical rather than nonphysical phenomena. Nevertheless, one of the best-known biologists, Alfred Kinsey (1894-1956), drew numerous subjective conclusions from his biased research in human sexuality. Kinsey had been highly influenced by Charles Darwin's evolution ideas, which helped him decimate traditional sexual morality. In fact, the sexual revolution may never have occurred without Darwin's theory of evolution, in which he postulated that all species of life evolved over a period of time. By the late nineteenth century, the scientific community and many of the general public had accepted evolution as a fact, even without substantial physical proof. Moreover, evolution obviously contradicts the biblical teachings of creation.

Since that time, many evolutionists in various fields have used Darwin's "science falsely so called" and applied it to the human condition, thereby contributing to anti-biblical morality. In his article "Kinsey, Darwin and the Sexual Revolution," Jerry Bergman asserts:

> Alfred Kinsey is the father of the modern Western sexual revolution. A review of the life and work of Kinsey reveals Darwinism was critically important in his crusade to overturn traditional sexual morality. He tried achieving this goal by convincing the public and the scientific world that what was widely regarded as deviant behavior then, including adultery, fornication, homosexuality, sadomasochism and paedophilia, were all widely practiced and therefore "normal" and acceptable. Kinsey's conclusions have now been shown by extensive empirical research to be fatally flawed. **Kinsey's sexual revolution has caused major social problems, an epidemic**

of disease and the breakdown of the family.[25] (Bold added.)

When individuals base their thinking and beliefs on evolution, the truth of God as creator is either erased or penciled over with the notion that God somehow had to use evolution in order to create His universe. In reality, one faith replaced another, and evolutionary morality based on animal behavior replaced biblical morality. **In other words, sexual immorality replaced the morality of God's created order, and particularly God's sexual design.**

Kinsey's most influential books are *Sexual Behavior in the Human Male*[26] and *Sexual Behavior in the Human Female.*[27] These books brought sexuality front and center and engendered interest in sex and its many possible variations. However, Kinsey's research was not without controversy because of his choice to use for his data base individuals who did **not** represent the average American man or woman. Nevertheless, in spite of serious flaws in his research, Kinsey was hailed as an expert on sexology. His teaching and writing turned the minds of many and prepared Americans to change their attitudes about sex and sexual behaviors.

Kinsey's own personal sexual preferences no doubt influenced much of his research and particularly his research conclusions. He, himself, was bisexual. It is reported that "as a young man, [he] would punish himself for having homoerotic feelings."[28] Kinsey and his wife "agreed that both could have sex with other people as well as with each other. He had sex with other men, including his student."[29]

Dr. Paul Cameron notes some serious problems with Kinsey's research. He says: "Kinsey's sampling method was woefully defective; heavily overloaded with prisoners, gay bars, and prostitutes; completely non-random." He further says that Kinsey presented a "distorted picture of American sexual habits" and "severely overestimated the prevalence of homosexuality."[30] Thus Kinsey's claims about arriving at "statistically common behavior" were deceptive because of his choice of interviewees. Instead of using a cross-sample of individuals across the country, Kinsey used prisoners and other "biased groups." Vern L. Bullough, in his book *Sexual Variance in Society and History*, says in reference to population groups with a paucity of members of the opposite sex: "We know, for example, that more homosexuality exists in prisons than outside."[31]

Even before the publication of Kinsey's *Male Report*, the media had picked up the following statistics regarding his findings, not realizing that they were untrustworthy:

- 85% of males in the U.S. have intercourse prior to marriage.

- Nearly 70% have sex with prostitutes.

- Between 30% and 45% of husbands have extra-marital intercourse.

- 37% of all males have homosexual experiences between adolescence and old age.[32]

These statistics were quite a surprise to the ordinary American. They brought great confusion regarding the traditional views and values and opened the door to all kinds of perverse sexual behavior, **with the misunder-standing that abnormal was normal and what had been considered normal had actually been abnormal.** Cameron points out that Kinsey's claims that "37% of all men" have participated in homosexuality and "10% were more or less homosexual" are in gross error—a myth that continues to be perpetrated by gay activists. Cameron gives the "Best Evidence Today" as "<2% of adults are currently 'homosexual' in large-scale probability surveys."[33]

Kinsey, together with three other like-minded colleagues wrote "Concepts of Normality and Abnormality," in which they blame religious moral codes for restricting sodomy and other sexual practices and lifestyles of homosexuals. They say: "With the expansion of the temporal power of the Christian Church, the control of the whole body of sex law and custom fell into religious hands, and remained there for many centuries."[34] They further say:

> The enforcement of these fundamentally religious codes against the so-called sexual perversions has been accomplished, throughout the centuries, by attaching considerable emotional significance to them. This has been effected, in part, by synonymizimg the terms clean, natural, normal, moral, and right, and the terms unclean, unnatural, abnormal, immoral, and wrong.[35]

Kinsey et al. blame Christian moral codes for harming those individuals who have homosexual desires by making them feel guilty for their "natural" feelings. In other words, they reject what the Bible says and contend that its restrictions have nothing to do with what is right or wrong sexually for what they refer to as the "human animal." They say that to determine what is normal and abnormal for the human animal one must take into consideration "the sexual behavior of man's primate relatives, and that of mammals in general."[36]

Kinsey et al. contend that all sexual attractions and practices that are similar to other mammals are normal. They conclude their chapter by saying:

> In the light of these accumulated data, we must conclude that current concepts of normality and abnormality in human sexual behavior represent what are **primarily moral evaluations**. They have little if any biologic justification. The problem presented by the so-called sexual perversions is a product of the disparity between the basic biologic heritage of the human animal, and the **traditional, cultural codes**.[37] (Bold added.)

In other words, the disparity in what is right and wrong depends in part on whether one has **faith in evolution or Creation: faith in Darwin or God.**

Kinsey is a booming anti-Christian voice from "science falsely so-called" that promoted transforming abnormal (against nature) to normal. Dr. Judith A. Reisman and Edward W. Eichel, in their book, *Kinsey, Sex and Fraud: The Indoctrination of a People*, say:

> No man in modern times has shaped public attitudes to, and perceptions of, human sexuality more than the late Alfred C. Kinsey. **He advocated that all sexual behaviors considered deviant were normal, while polemicizing that**

exclusive heterosexuality was abnormal and a product of cultural inhibitions and societal conditioning.... Few people realized that the data he presented were not, as claimed, scientific. Nor were the data representative of societal norms.... The importance of this issue is underscored by the fact that Kinsey's conclusions have become, to some extent, a self-fulfilling prophecy. They are the basis for much that is taught in sex education and for an ongoing agenda to engineer public attitudes about human sexuality.[38] (Bold added.)

Emancipation and Equality for Sexual Freedom

A series of human rights movements designed to set people free from oppression inadvertently contributed to the sexual rights agenda. We are thankful for all that has been done to free Blacks from slavery and prejudice and to grant equal rights to people of all races and creeds. We are thankful that women are more and more being treated fully as human beings. However, the push for women's rights in tandem with the sexual revolution led to women wanting an equal right to engage in sex without the burden of pregnancy. The first solution to the problem of pregnancy was birth control. It has been said, "Perhaps if the pill had not been invented, American politics would be very different today.... The Pill made possible the sexual revolution of the 1960s."[39]

In 1960 the FDA approved the first oral contraceptive, the birth control pill.[40] Although "the pill" was not immediately available by law in all states, approximately 1,187,000 women were using it by 1962.[41] However, if birth control failed, the woman, but not the man, would bear the consequence of pregnancy and child bearing. Many women did not want those consequences and pushed for so-called rights over their own bodies. In 1973 the Supreme Court's landmark decision in Roe v. Wade permitted a woman under certain conditions to have an abortion.[42] Somehow these women who aborted were led to believe that the fetus was part of their own body, but not truly a human being.

Following the righteous cause for equal rights for people of all races and creeds and the unrighteous cause to legalize the right to kill one's own unborn baby, another group surfaced in fighting for minority rights. Homosexual activists placed themselves in a category of deserving equal rights with a twist. They wanted the right to have their sexual preferences and activities considered normal and good. But, first they had to get rid of the anti-Sodomy laws that were in place in 1960 and which carried possible imprisonment for anyone participating in sodomy (oral and/or anal sex).

The Stonewall riots of 1969 are considered to be a pivotal rallying point in leading to the gay liberation movement.[43] Homosexual activists worked assiduously state by state to have such laws changed. However, sodomy was not legalized in all 50 states until 2003.[44] Although in some States these laws were against all sodomy, whether practiced by homosexuals or heterosexuals, in practice they were only used against homosexuals, which, of course, was unfair and discriminatory. It is not their private sexual rights that concern us. It is their public demands for minority rights that deeply concern us. As we shall see in the next chapter, their progress towards the acceptance of homosexual sexual practices have accelerated to the point of sodomy (oral and anal sex) being considered natural and normal and even, by many Christians, a pleasurable gift from God.

Calling Evil Good and Good Evil

Homosexuality was listed as a mental disorder prior to 1973, but it was removed from the *Diagnostic and Statistical Manual of Mental Disorders* (*DSM*) by vote. An article in *The American Journal of Psychiatry* explains how the controversy was fully resolved in the *DSM-III* to make it normal unless a homosexual person feels uncomfortable with his homosexual orientation to the point of seeking psychiatric help.

> In 1973 homosexuality per se was removed from the *DSM-II* classificatio of mental disorders and replaced by the category Sexual Orientation Disturbance. This represented a compromise between the view that preferential homosexuality is invariably a mental disorder and the view that it is merely a normal sexual variant. [45]

Both the American Psychiatric Association and the American Psychological Association have bought into the idea that like-sex orientation is normal, if it feels normal, and that the sexual activities between like-sex individuals are also normal, if they feel normal. Worse yet, the American Psychiatric Association has gone on record to say that pedophilia is no longer a mental disorder unless it disturbs the person or brings harm to anyone else.[46]

The Media: Public Proclamation of Sexual Uncleanness and Fornication

Of course the sexual revolution was only the beginning. The leaven of the sexual revolution continued to expand both through advocacy groups and the media. The world entered every household, not just through the ears (radio), but through the eyes (television). Step by step divorce and fornication became more socially acceptable. Thus, in 1969 film director Andy Warhol (1928-1987) directed *Blue Movie*, the first sexually explicit "adult movie" to be released to movie theaters across America.[47] Again, that was just the beginning.

As we shall show in the next chapter, the leaven has continued to expand throughout America in ways that, at the beginning of the sexual revolution itself, would have been inconceivable. The expansion has been swift and unstoppable because of the dramatic shift from morality based outside self to a new relative morality, based inside self, that too often ends in immorality. As one historian noted, "the sexual revolution was a time of 'coming out': about premarital sex, masturbation, erotic fantasies, pornography use, and sexuality."[48]

Boas, Maslow, Benedict, Mead, Rand, Branden, Kinsey, and Warhol are all dead, but their pernicious, perverse legacy as to what is sexually normal lives on. They have vastly influenced our society to place itself under the curse of woes: "Woe unto them that call evil good, and good evil; that put darkness for light, and light for darkness; that put bitter for sweet, and sweet for bitter! Woe unto them that are wise in their own eyes, and prudent in their own sight! (Isa. 5:20-21).

4

The Sodomy
of Americans

Each generation, since the beginning of the sexual revolution, has moved further away from chastity and marital fidelity and further into self-love, self-satisfaction, self-gratification, and free fornication. What used to be considered unnatural is now looked upon as natural. For many, traditional sexual values and restraints are a thing of the past. And, for many of those who still believe in them, there is a stretching of the meaning of chastity and fidelity and a widening of sexual activities. Nevertheless, in the midst of ever-increasing sexual freedom and affluence, many are dissatisfied. They never find what they are really looking for, because lust is never satisfied

One underlying feature of the sexual revolution was narcissism, where self is central to everything: I will have my own way—I deserve what pleases me. The therapeutic gospel is all about self. Eva Moskowitz's book *In Therapy We Trust* is subtitled *America's Obsession with Self-Fulfillment*. Her main theme has to do with the "therapeutic gospel." She says:

> There are three central tenets to this "therapeutic gospel." The first is that happiness should be our supreme goal. Wealth, public recognition, high moral character—each of these achievements is held valuable only to the extent that it makes us happy. Success, in the final analysis, must be measured with a psychological yardstick….
>
> The second tenet of our therapeutic faith is the belief that our problems stem from psychological causes. Problems that were once considered political, economic, or educational are today found to be psychological….
>
> The third and final tenet of the therapeutic gospel is the most important, but it is so universally accepted, so seemingly self-evident, that we hardly notice its existence. This tenet is that the psychological problems that underlie our failures and unhappiness are in fact treatable and that we can, indeed *should*, address these problems both individually and as a society. This is the essence of the therapeutic gospel.[1] (Italics in original.)

Last-days lovers of self seek personal happiness as the supreme goal and the therapeutic gospel convinces people that unhappiness is "treatable."

One Nation Under Therapy, by Christina Hoff Sommers and Sally Satel, M.D., "demonstrates that 'talking about' problems is no substitute for confronting them."

The subtitle of the book reveals its contents: *How the Helping Culture Is Eroding Self-Reliance*. They say:

> Americans have traditionally placed great value on self-reliance and fortitude. In recent decades, however, we have seen the rise of a therapeutic ethic that views Americans as emotionally underdeveloped, psychically frail, and requiring the ministrations of mental health professionals to cope with life's vicissitudes. Being "in touch with one's feelings" and freely expressing them have become paramount personal virtues. Today—with a book for every ailment, a counselor for every crisis, a lawsuit for every grievance, and a TV show for every conceivable problem— we are at risk of degrading our native ability to cope with life's challenges.[2]

Narcissism, having begun in the Garden of Eden, has reached epidemic proportions to the point of personal entitlement. Authors Jean M. Twenge and W. Keith Campbell , in their book *The Narcissism Epidemic: Living in the Age of Entitlement*, describe what they call "the road of narcissism" as one of "greed, self-centeredness, shallow relationships, vanity, social isolation, phony economics, bailouts, and blame."[3] They say:

> We went from an independent but community-oriented culture to one that can accept, without irony, the idea that admiring oneself is all-important, and believes that self-centeredness is necessary for success in life. These changes were not imposed by a dictator, imperial fiat, or religious decree. Instead, the changes built of themselves

slowly, so that they seem a natural part of who we are.[4]

Twenge and Campbell ask the reader to "imagine narcissism in society resting on a four-legged stool" and say;

> One leg is developmental, including permissive parenting and self-esteem-focused education. The second leg is the media culture of shallow celebrity. The third is the Internet: Despite its many benefits, the Web also serves as a conduit for individual narcissism. Finally easy credit makes narcissistic dreams into reality…. Each of these "legs" supports living in a narcissistic fantasy instead of in reality.[5]

Unless there is a turnaround, the narcissism epidemic and its accompanying disregard for God, His Word, and His design for sexual intimacy will continue on with an ever expansion of Paul's prophecy in his second letter to Timothy:

> This know also, that in the last days perilous times shall come. For men shall be lovers of their own selves, covetous, boasters, proud, blasphemers, disobedient to parents, unthankful, unholy, without natural affection, trucebreakers, false accusers, incontinent, fierce, despisers of those that are good, traitors, heady, highminded, lovers of pleasures more than lovers of God (2 Tim. 3:1-4).

The Lord God created the man and the woman for each other. All are called to love one another, even sacrificiall . However, when it comes to sexual intimacy, the Bible is explicit about sexual union, as we describe earlier in Chapters 1 and 2. Nevertheless, as paganism in all its forms, including atheism and agnosticism, moves in the direction of participation and support for sexual practices contrary to the Creator's sexual design, America is moving rapidly in the downward spiral of Romans 1:18-32 (see Chapter 2), which clearly shows the subsequent progression of a society that does not honor God as God and that will follow its own sinful inclinations.

Same-Sex Sexual Activities and Their Use by Heterosexuals

The consequences of the sexual revolution continue to evolve with increasing openness about a wide variety of sexual practices and much experimentation. Instead of discretion in describing sexual activities, there has been an avalanche of unnecessary details. Alfred Kinsey wanted everyone to know all avenues of sexual stimulation from his own personal fornicating and from his interviews with persons who were open to share their bizarre sexual practices. Verbal and visual guides to such practices became available and, although some people were horrified, others became quite curious. Then curiosity merged into a lust for more and more details and experimentation. What homosexuals did privately with each other came out into the open and entered the bedrooms of heterosexual couples, and that included Christian couples as well, which we describe in the next chapter.

Same-sex sexual practices stretch back to early times. The Bible does not mention such practices prior to the record of Sodom and Gomorrah. However, one can infer from the Genesis account that such practices were not new to Sodom and Gomorrah, but rather accompanied the other sins therein as a result of the Fall in the Garden. Ancient records reveal that sexual relationships between men and between men and young boys constituted an accepted part of many societies.[6] Other societies discriminated and yet others made such men shamans or priests (as well as male prostitutes).[7] One can generalize to say that such practices could be freely found in pagan cultures to some degree and in some form.

In this section we give a brief description of what men do sexually with men and women do sexually with each other in their love-making. We hope to be discrete and yet clarify what same-sex partners do with each other in addition to kissing and caressing, with the understanding that the Bible is clear about all forms of fornication, which would include all sexual activities outside God's design for sexual intimacy between a man and woman within the oneness of marriage:

> But fornication, and all uncleanness, or covetousness, let it not be once named among you, as becometh saints…. Let no man deceive you with vain words: for because of these things cometh the wrath of God upon the children of disobedience. Be not ye therefore partakers with them…. And have no fellowship with the unfruitful works of darkness, but rather reprove them. For it is a shame even to speak of those things which are done of them in secret. But all things that are reproved are made manifest by the light: for whatsoever doth make manifest is light. (Eph. 5:3, 5-6, 11-13.)

Although we resist speaking "of those things which are done of them in secret," we must give some information as light to show forth what "things are reproved" according to God's Word.

Because same-sex partners do not have the complementary body parts for godly sexual intercourse, which is the insertion of a man's penis into a woman's vagina, other ways have been invented as substitutes. These substitute ways are primarily oral and anal sex, in which the penis is inserted into the partner's mouth or anus and other combinations with the mouth, anus, and genitals. These are substitutes that violate God's original design for sex.

According to a statistical analysis, oral sex is practiced by all homosexuals and is "probably the most commonly known of all the many homosexual acts."[8] Specificall , "cunnilingus is oral sex performed on a female, while fellatio is oral sex performed on a male."[9] In addition to oral sex, homosexuals regularly engage in anal sex. One compilation of statistics indicates that 93 percent of homosexuals practice anal intercourse.[10] This and other homosexual practices will be named later on with their potential horrible and even lethal consequences.

Increasing acceptance of sexual deviation has reached the point at which heterosexual sex often includes homosexual activities, both within and outside marriage. We use the word "deviation," because all of these practices deviate from God's intent and sexual design of coital intercourse between one man and one woman in a committed marital relationship. Although there are many perverse sexual activities between like-sex individuals, oral and anal sex are the primary ones being adopted by heterosexuals. Thanks to Kinsey, the media, and homosexual activists, heterosexuals have not only tried these deviations from God's design, but amp up their sex through adding them to their repertoire. But, once people move away from God's sexual design, they become entrapped by the wiles of the devil and find that they need increasingly more out-of-the-ordinary forms of sexual stimulation.

How Moral Decline Broke the Sodomy Barrier

American morality has moved from its previous Christian influence to humanistic subjectivism, wherein external values and restraints are rejected and replaced with whatever seems right or wrong to an individual at any particular moment. This dramatic shift can be seen in the results of a LifeWay Research survey, which they conducted for Ligonier Ministries:

> One of the most troubling findings in the survey is the lack of understanding Americans have regarding sin and the total depravity of human beings. Actually the majority of Americans perceive goodness to be a better description of people.... 67% agree "Everyone sins at least a little, but most people are by nature good."[11]

The sexual revolution led to increasing moral decline in this country and broke the sodomy barrier. In his article "The Sodomizing of Our Churches," O. R. Adams says:

> Without the moral decline in this country, the homosexual movement could have made no progress, but the sexual revolution and the 1960s

moral decline paved the way for the success of that movement.... One professional organization after another caved in to the movement, including the American Psychological Association, the American Psychiatric Association, the American Medical Association, and even the American Bar Association. Academia, the news media, and the entertainment media were among the first to fall. The largest teachers' union, the National Education Association (NEA), became an arm of the homosexualists, and became involved in the indoctrinating of school children with propaganda that acts of sodomy were acceptable conduct, under the guise of sex education. Such "sex education" has always been an important tool of the homosexual movement.[12]

Many Americans are supporting homosexual activities because they, themselves, are involved in various forms of uncleanness and fornication. Websites for "hookups" abound. They offer sexual excitement for those who are looking for homosexual or heterosexual sexual relationships outside marriage with the idea that there is nothing wrong with such activities. In short, they are match-making services for homosexual and heterosexual fornication. Some such sites give married persons the availability to sin against their spouse in secret and without shame—that is, until hackers expose the lists of participants, which we will discuss in the next chapter.[13]

As heterosexuals have loosened their standards, many have incorporated homosexual activities. A national survey conducted by the U.S. Department of Health and Human Services revealed:

> Among adults aged 25-44, about 98% of women and 97% of men ever had vaginal intercourse, 89% of women and 90% of men ever had oral sex with an opposite-sex partner, and 36% of women and 44% of men ever had anal sex with an opposite-sex partner.[14]

As heterosexuals become engaged in oral and anal sex themselves, they become more open to the idea of homosexuality being normal. After all, they are doing the same things! **The sequence is this: the practice of homosexual acts of oral and/or anal sex by heterosexuals opened the door to swallowing the whole homosexual agenda.** God's sexual design is coitus within heterosexual marriage. It's the only kind of sex by which a couple can have a child. It is God's design for sexual procreation and pleasure, no matter how people may want to justify what they are doing sexually.

With the sexual revolution having broken down the barriers that used to exist, homosexual activities are easily accepted, ignored, or tolerated by most of society. As heterosexuals are fornicating at an increasing rate, with more and more heterosexuals living in sexual relationships prior to marriage or for however long they decide to stay together, who could be concerned about the sexual practices of anybody else? In fact, a recent survey indicated that "Americans are more accepting of gay relationships and couples living together before marriage—but they've grown less comfortable with divorce."[15]

Secular books and videos describing and demonstrating a wide variety of possible sexual activities and toys are big sellers as they encourage readers and viewers to try something new to enhance their sexual excursions into ever-increasing nuances. Most of these new activities and new toys have their origin in homosexual sexual activities, which are substitutes for God's sexual design for procreation with pleasure, because homosexuals are unable to perform coital intercourse with each other.

Heterosexuals performing these homosexual sexual acts are increasingly publicized, with examples of people in high places engaging in oral sex without a hint of embarrassment, aside from being caught. Heterosexual oral sex was blatantly revealed in the former President Bill Clinton scandal. In fact, Clinton denied having sex with the young female since there was no coital sex. Moreover, numerous heterosexual couples, whether married or not, engage in oral sex as a form of birth control. So, if everybody is doing it, people believe that it must be okay and that no one should look askance at such practices, whether performed between same-sex couples or hetero-sex couples.

The Influence of Pornograph

Add pornography to the mix with its ready online availability and its addictive facets, whereby the more one does it, the more one lusts for more at a more intense dose, just like with drugs. Neuroscience reveals: "The surging of dopamine from viewing porn eventually subsides, leaving the person wanting more. More novel and intense pornography is then needed to achieve the same excitement as before."[16]

As Mary Sykes Wylie notes in her article "The Unspeakable Language of Sex," "While in America in 1991 fewer than 90 different adult magazines were being published, by 2010 or so, there were 2.5 million adult web-sites, catering to every taste, imaginable and unimaginable."[17] Pornography pops up everywhere on the internet where it is amply available, accessible, affordable (free), anonymous, and addictive. The internet has indeed become a venue for secret sin that enslaves the souls of its victims.

Statistics on pornography may not be completely accurate because of the ways polling might be done. However, one website posts a number of shocking statistics from a compilation of numerous polls, which indicate in their extensive list that "72 million internet users visit pornography web sites per year" and "70% of 18-to-24-year-old men visit pornographic sites in a typical month. 66% of men in their 20s and 30s also report being regular users of pornography." They include one poll that reports: "47.48 percent of families said pornography is a problem in their home." In addition to the internet, "There are 800 million rentals each year of adult videos and DVDs" and "Half of all hotel guests order pornographic movies."[18]

Research reported in *Surgical Neurology International* reveals that pornography is not only addictive; it changes the brain. The researchers say:

> The sex industry has successfully characterized any objection to pornography as being from the religious/moral perspective; they then dismiss these objections as First Amendment infringements. If pornography addiction is viewed objectively, evidence indicates that it does indeed cause harm in humans with regard to pair-bonding. The correlation (85%) between viewing child pornography and participating in actual sexual rela-

tions with children was demonstrated by Bourke and Hernandez. The difficulty in objective peer-reviewed discussion of this topic is again illustrated by the attempted suppression of this data on social grounds. The recent meta-analysis by Hald *et al.* strongly supports and clarifies previous data demonstrating correlation with regard to pornography inducing violent attitudes against women. With such strong correlative data, it is irresponsible not to address the likely possibility of causation in these regards. Reviewing this data in the context of current usage patterns is particularly concerning; 87% of college age men view pornography, 50% weekly and 20% daily or every other day, with 31% of women viewing as well. The predictive effect of pornography on sexual behavior in adolescents has also been demonstrated.[19]

Pornography enslaves men, wrecks marriages, and violates women whose husbands are lusting after the bodies of other women, while corrupting their own marital sex. Pornography participants become further lashed to lust and fornication, and they will accept almost anything and everything, except God and the Bible.

Egregious Education

Alfred Kinsey's legacy lives on to the ruination of America's children. In spite of his flawed research, numerous individuals believe his conclusions about sexual pleasure being good for everybody, including young children. Kinsey's corrupt ideas have permeated the schools through various organizations. Dr. Judith Reisman says;

Before Kinsey, home economics, health, or physical education teachers taught about menstruation, reproduction, and sometimes, marital behavior. From biology class to instruction on finances, these lessons taught that sex was good, but only in marriage, for reasons of health, happiness, and societal well-being. Simple…. But once Kinsey sexualized America's children from birth onward, school activists argued that their districts needed trained instructors—"experts"— to teach students about sex. Soon, classes that were euphemistically called "sex education," "family life," "health," "hygiene," "abstinence," or "diversity," "hate crimes" and, later, "AIDS awareness" infected most American schools.[20]

Two primary organizations contributing to sexual corruption are Planned Parenthood and SIECUS (Sex Information and Education Council of the United States), which was founded in 1964 by Dr. Mary S. Calderone, former Medical Director for the Planned Parenthood Federation.[21] Way back in 1953, Dr. Lena Levine wrote in *Planned Parenthood News* that the organization's goal was:

…to be ready as educators and parents to help young people obtain sex satisfaction before marriage. By sanctioning sex before marriage we will prevent fear and guilt. We must also relieve those who have these … feelings, and we must be ready to provide young boys and girls with the best contraceptive measures available so they will have the necessary means to achieve sexual

satisfaction without having to risk possible pregnancy.[22]

Children in various schools across the nation are being taught "safe sex," not only to avoid pregnancy, AIDS, and other STDs, but to know how to do it at an early age.[23]

Planned Parenthood has a number of resources for parents to teach their children about sex. Christian groups have expressed concern about the content. For example, Planned Parenthood includes in its resources a book for children ages 10 and up titled *It's Perfectly Normal: Changing Bodies, Growing Up, Sex, and Sexual Health* by Robie Harris[24] The book is highly graphic with drawings depicting nude people of all ages, sexual organs, intercourse, and masturbation. It gives a positive spin on homosexuality and invites children to decide for themselves what their sexuality is: gay, lesbian, or trans-gender.

Kinsey would be pleased the way information about various forms of sex is available through the schools and other media. Freud would also be pleased that "safe" sex without restraint is now available. In 2014 a report was published about "Chicago schools teaching 'safe' anal sex to 5th graders."[25] Fox News (2017) reports that *Teen Vogue* magazine "is defending its decision to publish a graphic tutorial to anal sex for children and teenagers—calling critics homophobic."[26] The news article by Todd Starnes quotes Gigi Engle, author of "A Guide to Anal Sex," as saying "Anal sex and anal stimulation can be awesome, and if you want to give it a go, you do that. More Power to you."[27] This kind of influence on children and teens through the years following the sexual revolution until today somewhat explain why so many people are in favor of sex before marriage, all forms of sexual pleasure, and homosexuality. How many Americans who are adults now have been influenced during their vulnerable years by misguided myths about sex that replace the Bible regarding morality, in general, and sexual purity in particular?

Increase in Same-Sex Sexual Practices

The sexual revolution, in tandem with an ever-expanding growth of personal entitlement, has led to an increase of same-sex practices and nearly wholesale acceptance of homosexuality. In 2016 Erin O'Flaherty made the news by becoming the first openly gay Miss Missouri and the first lesbian to compete for the Miss America title.[28] Not only are members of the homosexual community coming out; they are treated as heroes, and others are joining them through curiosity and ever-increasing lust for sexual experiences. The General Social Survey of U. S. Adults conducted from the years 1972-2014 asked questions regarding sexual activity between same-sex individuals. The subsequent analysis revealed a substantial increase in both attitude and practice.[29] After analyzing all the data, the researchers concluded:

> In a nationally representative survey of American adults, same-sex sexual experience has doubled, and acceptance has quadrupled. This suggests that the cultural change of the last few decades extends beyond simple tolerance of gay, lesbian, and bisexual individuals and their civil rights to include acceptance of same-sex sexuality and the freedom to engage in same-sex sexuality—or at

least the freedom to report one has done so on a survey. **Either way, Americans have experienced a fundamental shift toward acceptance of same-sex sexual behavior and a greater willingness to engage in it.**[30] (Bold added.)

While the "percentage of women who had sex with at least one other woman more than doubled between the early 1990s and the 2010s…and the percentage of men who had sex with at least one other man nearly doubled… across all eras, men who had sex exclusively with other men were 1.7% of the population, while women who had sex exclusively with other women were .9% of the population."[31] Thus, the reported increase has been among those practicing bisexual activity—engaging in sex with both sexes.

The researchers propose three reasons for the increase in same-sex sexual practices: (1) time period and the make-up of the population during the time period, with "the increased individualism" and a "cultural system that places more emphasis on the self and less on social rules" and with the accompanying changes in "social norms and values"; (2) "changes in policies and laws" giving a greater "perceived feasibility of same-sex partnerships"; (3) "recent changes in the visibility of gays and lesbians (and same-sex sexual behavior more generally…) and the popularity and increased use of online social and sexual networking to meet potential sex partners." They say "Finally, since the 1980s, bisexuality has become more visible and viable as an identity and behavior option, as evidenced by increased networking opportunities, scholarship around bisexuality, and bisexuality activism both within and outside of lesbian and gay activist circles."[32] We would add that positive visibility of same-sex sexual relationships in the media (internet, movies, television, articles, and books) has greatly infl - enced the changes in both attitudes and practice.

Notice how these social and behavior changes reflect Romans One. While all creation points to both the exis- tence and authority of God, those who did not glorify Him as God with thanksgiving "became vain in their imagina- tions, and their foolish heart was darkened" (Rom. 1:21). One of the observations made while examining the above data was that, during the same years, there was a decline in church attendance. In other words, fewer and fewer people honored God as God while more and more went their own way during the sexual revolution. Thus, "God also gave them up to uncleanness through the lusts of their own hearts, to dishonour their own bodies between themselves" (Rom. 1:24).

Another aspect found by the researchers was this: "most research indicates that same-sex sexual experience has increased more among women than men."[33] Perhaps that is why Paul, in writing to the Romans mentions the sinful sexual activity between women before the sinful sexual activity between men: "For this cause God gave them up unto vile affections: for even their women did change the natural use into that which is against nature: And likewise also the men, leaving the natural use of the woman, burned in their lust one toward another" (Rom. 1:26-27).

From Personal Sin to National Sin

From the beginning of the sexual revolution until now an increasing number of individuals in America have been violating God's design for sexual intercourse. However sex without personal restraints often leads to pregnancy in spite of the various methods designed to prevent it. As the fight for women's rights increased along with the sexual revolution, women cried out for the right to abort an "accidental" pregnancy. They wanted full rights over their own bodies with the idea that a fetus was not a person. This increasing demand for sexual freedom without consequences led to the national sin of legalizing abortion. Legalizing abortion was accomplished through the infamous Roe v. Wade decision by the Supreme Court of America. The United States granted females sexual freedom at the cost of almost 60 million unborn babies mutilated and murdered in the womb since 1973. [34]

As the homosexual activists joined forces, they gained the right to engage in homosexual practices, which had formerly been punishable by law. They worked on two fronts: the legal front and the social front. As mentioned in Chapter 3, the nation changed its laws regarding homosexuality so that by 2003 all of the States had removed their anti-sodomy laws. Also, as mentioned in Chapter 3, this law had been used unfairly against homosexuals and was therefore discriminatory. The laws of the land should apply to all without discrimination. However, we do want to report on the mind-set of Americans. The very change itself reveals a dramatic shift in the attitude of Americans about homosexual sexual practices, because the anti-sodomy laws showed that the nation and its citizens had once believed that sexual practices between members of the same sex were reprehensible. But, as Alfred Kinsey and the Sexual Revolution opened people's minds to all sorts of sexual deviancy, fewer and fewer people saw anything wrong with these acts. Thus on the social front, they gained acceptance.

Homosexuals and their supporters continued to work assiduously toward what they considered to be "equality" as they fought for the right to marry members of the same sex, in opposition to God's design for marriage to be only between a man and a woman. They succeeded and on June 26, 2015 the United States of America violated God's design for marriage and the family. On that date the Supreme Court of America ruled that homosexuals have the right to be married to each other. However, this cannot truly be an "equal rights" issue since they already had the same marriage right as everybody else, i.e., they already had the equal right to marry a person of the opposite sex. Instead of an "equal right," this is a special "right," which violates God's intention and creation. Moreover, this new "right" entails numerous concessions, which rob rights of those who believe God's Word regarding human sexuality and marriage.

Fewer and fewer voices are being raised against homosexuals engaging in sodomy, because so many heterosexuals are doing oral and/or anal sex as well. Therefore these homosexual practices are more and more considered normal and good; and thus homosexuality must also be seen as normal and good. Moreover, homosexual activists want to shut down all voices that may disagree with their claims that what they are doing sexually is normal and moral, even though their sexual activities violate God's sexual design, which is coital intercourse between a man and woman within the covenant of marriage. In muzzling those who do not agree with them, homosexual activists are declaring that their so-called rights must take precedence over the God-given rights of others in the areas of freedom of conscience, freedom of religion, and freedom of speech. What other so-called right takes away the rights of others as specified in The Bill of Rights either directly or indirectly? America is getting closer and closer to calling all expressions of sexual deviation from God's sexual design as good and all critical exposure of such sexual deviation from God's sexual design as being hate crimes. The national conscience is being seared.

Indeed, our country is in trouble as it has been sinking deeper and deeper into self-centeredness, entitlement, lust, and self-proclaimed victimhood. Homosexuals continue to gain favor and special status because of their assumed victimhood, which may appear plausible on the surface because of their sexual orientation and behavior having had been rejected and considered abnormal, as homosexuality had been included as a psychiatric disorder in the earlier editions of the *Diagnostic and Statistical Manual of Psychiatric Disorders* and only later removed by vote.[35] Because homosexuality had been looked upon psychiatrically as abnormal and some homosexuals had been unjustly mocked and scorned, those who sympathized with them took on their cause and joined the fight. Then as more and more homosexuals "came out," publicly admitting their homosexuality, friends and family members who loved them took up their cause as being a prejudiced-against minority, requiring special protection from those who would not agree that their sexual preferences and practices are normal and labeling them "homophobic."

Humanistic psychology has dwelt much on victimization. After all, if a child has been born good, any deviation from inborn goodness must have been caused by something outside self. Thus everyone is a victim from the moment of birth (unless cruelly decimated in the womb) and is entitled to a better life. In his book *A Nation of Victims: The Decay of the American Character*, Charles J. Sykes declares: "…it is almost impossible to debate any issue of weight without running up against the politics of victimization….This rush to declare oneself a victim cannot be accounted for solely in political terms. Rather it suggests a more fundamental transformation of American cultural values and notions of character and personal responsibility."[36] He further says:

> The ethos of victimization has an endless capacity not only for exculpating one's self from blame, washing away responsibility in a torrent of explanation—racism, sexism, rotten parents, addiction, and illness—but also for projecting guilt onto others.[37]

He uses a term "victimspeak" in the following statements, which are quite revealing, particularly when used to support the homosexual activists' sexual agenda.

> Victimspeak is the trigger that permits the unleashing of an emotional and self-righteous response to any perceived slight…. Victimspeak insists upon moral superiority and moral absolutism and thus tends to put an abrupt end to conversation…. Ironically, this style of linguistic bullying often parades under the banner of "sensitivity."[38]

> To be sensitive (in victimspeak) is not to argue or to reason but to feel, to attune one's response to another's sense of aggrievement. This politicized sensitivity (as distinct from decency, civility, and honesty) demands the constant adjustment of one's responses to the shifting and unpredictable demands of the victim. The greater the wounds, the louder the cries of injustice, the greater the demand for sensitivity—no matter how unreasonable.[39]

Of course Sykes affirms there are true victims, but insists that victimization "militates against ideas of equity, fairness, and process; its natural tone is one of assertion of prerogatives, a demand for reparations."[40]

Homosexual activists capitalize on being victims of society, since they are not yet getting all they think they are entitled to. They see themselves as victims of those who oppose or disagree with their sexual views and practices—especially those who speak out against such distortions of God's sexual design. They have identified themselves as victims along with those who have been marginalized because of race or creed, but their own sexual agenda actually victimizes people of creed who believe and speak forth what God has said about human sexuality.

Homosexual activists say they are a prejudiced against minority group. For example, homosexuals want the same special protections of law for employment and housing as African Americans, Asians, Latinos, and other such minority groups who are recognized by their color and/or national characteristics. Of course none of these minority groups could change their physical appearance or national characteristics. And, none of these minority groups could hide under their skin color and looks; neither, for example, could an African American hide or recover from being a Black.

Homosexuals are visible only when they choose to make themselves visible. If someone were asked to reveal the number of homosexuals he/she knows without their revealing it, he/she would not be able to tell you, because there is no external identifying mark of skin color or specific national characteristics. Unless a gay or lesbian identifies himself/herself by making it clear verbally, no one really knows the sexual orientation. Even waving a rainbow flag or belonging to a homosexual pride organization would not be a clear identification because fellow travelers, allies, and sympathizers wave and join.

The homosexual agenda of being accepted publically for who they are and what they do in private is furthered by the number of public figures who are highly regarded and much admired "coming out of the closet" as gay or lesbian. The bottom line is more acceptance of the homosexuals and of their sex acts being normal and, therefore, good.

The normalizing of same-sex sodomy acts became more and more acceptable as more as more Americans and even more and more Christians became doers of oral and anal sex. **The commonality of heterosexuals indulging in oral and anal sex along with the homosexuals opened the door for accepting sodomy as normal and good.** Once heterosexual Americans in large numbers and many Christians adopted the same homosexual sex acts, the more accepting they became of the whole homosexual agenda. **Once this sodomy**

barrier was crossed by numerous heterosexuals, the special minority rights for employment and housing followed and new "rights" were created for same-sex marriages and for the acceptance, support, and even celebration of families with like-sex parents.

These not-so-equal special rights demanded by homosexual activists will continue to develop until this country bows the knee to sexual freedom of every sort to the point of legalized pederasty (homosexual activity between an adult male and a minor). America is not only experiencing an increase in all forms of fornication, but now it supports transgenders (individuals determining their own gender identity apart from their DNA and birth gender). The latest at this point is the bathroom issue devised to protect transgenders from being embarrassed by allowing them to use the bathroom of their gender choice, regardless of whether they are originally male or female. Thus "equal rights" are given to a very tiny group at the expense of equal rights to the larger population. So people wonder, "What's next?" The sexual revolution continues to spin and where it goes is anyone's guess.

Cultural Demise

The Bible stands on its own as far as being a Christian's authoritative guide. It does not need research to support its truth claims. However, there is strong research that confirms the necessity for adhering to God's design for sexual relationship: one man and one woman uniting in an enduring monogamous relationship. After years of research into numerous ancient cultures, Joseph D. Unwin (1895-1936), a British ethnologist and social anthropologist at Oxford University and Cambridge University, wrote a book entitled *Sex and Culture*. Before coming to his conclusions, Unwin gathered a great deal of data from 86 different people groups (80 of which he identifies as uncivilized societies and 6 of which he identifies as civilized societies) [41] He explains:

> My inductive survey of civilized societies is limited to the Sumerians, Babylonians (to twentieth century B.C.), Hellenes, Romans, Anglo-Saxons, and English. I also make a few references to the Arabs (Moors), and a deductive suggestion about the Persians, Macedonians, Huns, and Mongols. When I speak of "civilized" societies I refer only to the following sixteen historical peoples: Sumerians, Babylonians, Egyptians, Assyrians, Hellenes (3), Persians, Hindus, Chinese, Japanese, Sassanids, Arabs (Moors), Romans, Teutons, and Anglo-Saxons (i.e. ourselves). According to my terminology any society not included in this list was 'uncivilized.'[42]

Unwin was looking for evidence to show the degree to which sexual permissiveness or restraint affected cultures throughout history. His investigation required a great deal of information, included in his over 710-page book. He was not a Christian, but found that **societies thrived better when the sexual relationships were monogamous and that they deteriorated as the sexual restraints were removed**. Regarding the societies he investigated, he says:

> These societies lived in different geographical environments; they belonged to different racial

stocks; but the history of their marriage customs is the same. In the beginning each society had the same ideas in regard to sexual regulations. Then the same struggles took place; the same sentiments were expressed; the same changes were made ; the same results ensued. Each society reduced its sexual opportunity to a minimum and, displaying great social energy, flourished greatly. Then it extended its sexual opportunity; its energy decreased, and faded away. The one outstanding feature of the whole story is its unrelieved monotony.[43]

In surveying the facts he found:

1. that when they began to display great social energy the societies had reduced their sexual opportunity by the adoption of absolute monogamy;

2. that in each case the society was dominated by the group which displayed the greatest relative energy;

3. that as soon as the sexual opportunity of the society, or of a group within the society, was extended, the energy of the society, or of the group within it, decreased and finally disappeared

4. that whatever the racial extraction of the people, and whatever the geographical environment in which they lived, the manner in which they modified their absolute monogamy was the same in every case.[44]

He notes:

> **Thus it seems to be true that, just as a decrease of sexual opportunity produces a cultural advance, so an increase results in a cultural decline**. And, basing my conclusions on the same kind of evidence, I consider that the finest period of Mayan history was already past when the white man arrived in Central America, for it seems that among the Mayans also the demand for pre-nuptial chastity had been relaxed.[45] (Bold added.)

Everyone should pay attention to what Unwin found, because history repeats itself. The following could happen here as well:

> **The group within the society which suffered the greatest continence displayed the greatest energy, and dominated the society**. When absolute monogamy was preserved only for a short time, the energy was only expansive, but when the rigorous tradition was inherited by a number of generations the energy became productive. As soon as the institution of modified monogamy, that is, marriage and divorce by mutual consent, became part of the inherited tradition of a complete new generation, the energy, either of the whole society or of a group within the society, decreased, and then disappeared.[46] (Bold added.)

After conducting all his research, Unwin clearly saw the absolute importance of one man and one woman forming a family unit within an enduring monogamous relationship. In an article titled "Monogamy as a Condition of Social Energy," Unwin declared:

The whole of human history does not contain a single instance of a group becoming civilized unless it has been absolutely monogamous, nor is there any example of a group retaining its culture after it has adopted less rigorous customs.[47] (Bold added.)

From the American Dream to America's Demise

Unwin's research demonstrates the importance of absolute monogamy for a strong civilization and how cultures deteriorate when they move away from absolute monogamy to sexual permissiveness. He saw that when cultures move in this direction, they are deceived into thinking that they are progressing onward and upward to a better society, just as the numerous movers and shakers of our own sexual revolution no doubt thought they were advancing society. Unwin comments on this false sense of confidence

> Then, convinced that the cultural process is a progressive development and that our own culture is the most developed of all cultures, we assume that every change in our cultural condition is evidence of higher cultural development. Anything which is subsequent in time is regarded as more enlightened and more developed.[48]

Indeed, most American citizens believe that we are involved in a great cultural advance in every area. Advances in health, medicine, technology, and affluence can be deceptive, even while there has been an increase in such conditions as depression and other mental distresses. What can be wrong? God has blessed this country for many years and He is longsuffering, but the consequences of outright disobedience to His sexual design for mankind will eventually come to fruition, both personally and nationally. Rather than viewing sexual freedom as a blessing, this country needs to recognize it as a curse, described in Romans 1:18-32 and 2 Timothy 3:1-5.

God promised that He would not destroy mankind again with a world-wide Flood (Gen. 8:21-22). However, His patience did finally run out with Sodom and Gomorrah, and he erased them from the face of the earth, except for Lot and his family. **One would have to be spiritually blind not to see the similarity between the spiritual and sexual degradation that existed in Sodom and Gomorrah and the spiritual and sexual deterioration in America. Add up the current national sins in America: Darwinian evolution, the sexual revolution, abortion (Roe v. Wade), same sex marriages (Obergefell v. Hodges), disregard for God, rising narcissism (2 Tim. 3:2-5), and widespread sodomy. Many in America do not want this country to be "one Nation under God." Once that happens, the many blessings showered on America by God will disappear, which could lead to its demise.**

5

The Sodomy of Christians

The Sexual Revolution in America changed Americans' ideas about sex and their concomitant practices. Boundaries were not only broadened; in some cases they were obliterated. Then, as the world was opening itself up to an expansion of fornication, Christians gradually began to capitulate. However, when a person's belief conflicts with what one has begun doing, cognitive dissonance occurs, and the person is likely to change the belief to conform to the practice. As Christians began to indulge in the sexual practices unleashed upon the world, they adjusted their understanding of the Bible in order not to feel guilty.

Christians may be a bit slow in adopting the world's ways, but, once they do, they generally alter their understanding of Scripture to the point that what they copied from the world becomes sanctified in their own minds, even the practice of sodomy (oral and anal sex). In Chapter 4 we reported the results of a LifeWay Research survey that says: "One of the most troubling findings in the survey is the lack of understanding Americans have regarding sin and the total depravity of human beings."[1]

Homosexual sexual practices have been around for eons, but Kinsey is the one who, through his biased, hocus pocus science, convinced the entire nation that all forms of sex were being practiced by great numbers of variously gendered people, thus making homosexual sexual practices seem to be the norm for the nation. Through Kinsey's abracadabra of "science falsely so called," what had been privately practiced by homosexuals was adopted by heterosexuals and then publicly proclaimed as normal.

Kinsey's highly publicized mumbo-jumbo research results proclaimed that the use of homosexual sexual practices of oral, anal, and other non-coital sexual indulgences were being prolifically practiced and preferred by a high percentage of heterosexual Americans. Beneath the guise of science, Kinsey made sodomy seem acceptable. It must be okay if everyone is doing it, and those not doing it might wonder if they might be missing out on something great. Through extensive media coverage, what had been heretofore regarded as taboo and sinful, became normal, natural, and national.

Eventually the normal and natural sodomy conclusion about what was orthodoxly considered sinful invaded the church through Christians who were themselves engaging in oral and/or anal sex and enjoying it. The yeast of sodomy soon spread as more Christians shifted their beliefs about sexual purity to accommodate their oral and/or anal sex. As noted in Chapter 3, Kinsey was himself bisexual in preference and practice. Naturally he strove to make what he, himself, was doing appear to be the norm: what better way than to entice heterosexual men to indulge? And what better way for Satan, himself, to entice Christian men into sodomizing their wives.

The very act of heterosexuals engaging in oral and anal sex was a primary deciding factor in breaking down barriers that existed nationally between heterosexuals and homosexuals. Heterosexuals emulating homosexuals' sexual practices of sodomy eventually led to accepting the homosexual sexual agenda in the country and in much of the church.

Sex Surveys and What They Reveal

We cite a few surveys in the prior chapter because they can be useful in looking at trends in society. However, survey results can be faulty and even biased. One has to consider the purpose of the study, the questions themselves (are they leading, too ambivalent, or so controversial that they will elicit a false response?), the cohort (the population surveyed), how the survey is conducted, and the analysis of the results. For instance, if 90% admit to a particular behavior, one has to ask 90% of what population group? How might the results be skewed when the participants volunteer to take the survey? In such a case, this is already a select group. Therefore in citing survey results, we must keep in mind the population that was surveyed. In addition, survey-takers are often self-biased, which distorts the results.

As mentioned in Chapter 2, Kinsey surveyed prisoners regarding their sexual practices and put the results forth as though he had surveyed the general population. We mention this so that our readers will not take survey results as absolutes. **Nevertheless, the following survey**

results do reveal four trends in America and in the church that are of great concern: moral absolutes, sexual practices, pornography, and a growing acceptance of homosexuality.

Trends among Christians Regarding Moral Absolutes

A recent Barna study, described in "The End of Absolutes: America's New Moral Code," reveals not only the changing morals in society, but also among Christians:

> Christian morality is being ushered out of American social structures and off the cultural main stage, leaving a vacuum in its place—and the broader culture is attempting to fill the void. New research from Barna reveals growing concern about the moral condition of the nation, even as many American adults admit they are uncertain about how to determine right from wrong. So what do Americans believe? Is truth relative or absolute? And do Christians see truth and morality in radically different ways from the broader public, or are they equally influenced by the growing tide of secularism and religious skepticism?[2]

One can see the influence of secular humanism, as 91% of "All Adults" and 76% of "Practicing Christians" "somewhat" or "completely" agreed with the statement: **"The best way to find yourself is by looking within yourself"** (bold added).[3] The question itself is a reflection of the current centrality of self. We were not surprised at the 91% for all adults, but that 76% of Christians would look within themselves rather than to God and His Word reveals a shift into secular humanism among professing Christians. How easy it is to pick up the ideas of the world, perhaps without realizing it.

In response to the statement "The highest goal in life is to enjoy it as much as possible," 84% of "All Adults" and 67% of "Practicing Christians" "somewhat" or "completely" agreed.[4] What, indeed, are "Practicing Christians" if their highest goal is not to "glorify God" and "enjoy Him forever"? If the "highest goal in life is to enjoy it as much as possible," that means that they love pleasure more than they love God (2 Tim. 3:4). One can see why there has been a moral decline in the church.

In response to the statement "Any kind of sexual expression between two consenting adults is acceptable," 69% of "All Adults" and 30% of "Practicing Christians" "somewhat" or "completely" agreed.[5] While not as many "Practicing Christians" agreed with those statements, the percentage that did agree indicates that the world is ensconced in the church and **many professing Christians have succumbed to being of the world as well as in it**.

Fornication is definitely on the rise with the numerous hook-up sites discussed in the prior chapter. These appeal to Christians as well as nonChristians to the extent that, when one of the sites was hacked, numerous Christian men were among those who were outed, including church leaders and pastors, with a pastor and a seminary professor committing suicide as a result of their exposure.[6]

Trends Among Christians Regarding Sexual Practices

One survey aimed at Christian women, reported in *Today's Christian Woman* in 2008, asked a number of questions about sexual satisfaction. The early questions prepared the survey-takers for the final more probing-into-sexual-privacy questions under the heading "On the Wild Side." The first question, "Do you and your spouse have oral sex?" brought the following responses:

5% Did once

38% Did more than once

40% Do Regularly

17% Have not done at all[7]

The percentages in response to the question "Do you and your spouse have anal sex?" were:

11% Did once

11% Did more than once

1% Do Regularly

77% Have not done at all[8]

Many of the women were no doubt too embarrassed to answer these questions honestly, especially if they were participating in behavior they considered "nasty" and/or dishonoring to God. And, remember this: **surveys that ask uncomfortable or controversial questions on taboo subjects often elicit false responses**. As with such surveys, the actual numbers are generally significantly higher. The fact that the survey was done years ago is very telling, and the number of popular Christian books promoting at least oral sex and sometimes anal sex, which have been available in the interim, leads to the conclusion that the numbers of Christians practicing oral and anal sex have been on the rise since then.

Trends among Christians Regarding Pornography

The graphics of pornography, which were previously limited to "obscene writings, drawings, photographs or the like, esp. those having little or no artistic merit," first expanded to film and now promiscuously pervade the internet with its enticing lures to lust. Pornography in its etiology comes from the Greek words translated "porno," meaning harlot, and "graph" The word pornography itself first referred to "writing about harlots."[9] However, the obscene writings and pictures were around long before the coinage of the word. Pornography usage increased during the sexual revolution of the 1960s and exploded during the age of the internet.

More and more Christians are losing their biblical and moral bearings and succumbing to the enticing obscene graphics, which are "in your face" all over the internet. Many Christian men, including pastors, leaders, and seminary professors, and some Christian women have become regular users of pornography, which is a visual, mental form of fornication, as Jesus revealed in Matthew 5:28: "But I say unto you, That whosoever looketh on a woman to lust after her hath committed adultery with her already in his heart." As individuals put obscene sexual practices into their hearts and minds, they are more likely to participate in sodomy (oral and anal sex) and other non-coital forms of sexual gratification

One of the most significant tools used by Satan is the Internet with its World Wide Web. Although there are many positive, productive, and essential uses of the Web, it is also a repository of mountains of pornography, including an extensive variety of sexual activities, which open the whole world to viewing and voyeurism. Pornography, including sex acts, on the internet have been the source of ruined lives and wrecked marriages and has led to the spiritual decline of many Christians. Believers are going online with their phones, watches, tablets, and laptops. They are watching and listening to the ubiquitous media, with its vast means of communication, including the internet, radio, television, newspapers, movies, books, and magazines. The cacophony is a catastrophe for the many Christians who view, pursue, and practice the oral and/or anal sex of the homosexuals.

As mentioned earlier, surveys are helpful in showing trends among groups of people. However, they are vulnerable to flaws inherent in the survey questions, the participant selection, and the high possibility of false answers, as well as the original intent of the survey and the final analysis. Nevertheless, we will cite some of the conclusions to show that Christian men and women are involved in pornography. Interestingly, a number of sites reporting survey results advertise their services to Christians who believe they are addicted to pornography. Their percentages of pornography users are generally higher than some of the others, perhaps because of the choice of participants.

In 2001 *Christianity Today* conducted a survey of its readers regarding the use of internet pornography. At that time "33 percent of the clergy and 36 percent of laity" responded that they had "visited a sexually explicit Web site" and "18 percent of clergy said they visit sexually explicit Web sites between a couple of times a month and more than once a week."[10] That was back in 2001. The numbers have simply increased, as can be seen in a 2014 Barna study that was reported in an article on OneNews-Now.com, which said:

> **Christian men are having an alarmingly difficult time abstaining from the sexual sins of viewing pornography and committing adultery on their spouses, according to a new national survey. Tragically, married Christian men are failing miserably when it comes to these sins, as 55 percent look at pornography at least once a month and 35 percent cheated on their spouses in an extramarital affair.** (Bold in original.)

The percentages increase as the age decreases, as "77 percent of Christian men between the ages of 18 and 30 view pornography at least monthly, and 36 percent look at it at least once a day."[11]

Perhaps even more alarming are the results from a 2016 Barna study:

- **Most pastors (57%) and youth pastors (64%) admit they have struggled with porn, either currently or in the past.**

- Overall, 21% of youth pastors and 14% of pastors admit they currently struggle with using porn.

- About 12% of youth pastors and 5% of pastors say they are addicted to porn.

- 87% of pastors who use porn feel a great sense of shame about it.

- 55% of pastors who use porn say they live in constant fear of being discovered.[12]

Christian men are not the only ones who view and become addicted to pornography. An article in a Christian magazine titled "Women and Pornography Today," written by Marnie C. Ferree, who counsels Christian women who are addicted to sex, says, "The ubiquitous digital landscape has ushered today's women into the darkness of online pornography just as much as it has captured men."[13] She also refers to the same 2016 Barna study mentioned above, which found that "33% of women, ages 13-24 seek out porn at least once a month compared to 12% of women over age 25."[14]

Although the numbers are not as high, the very fact that women, who are usually more relational than lusting for the physical, are even interested in pornography reveals how far many Christians are sinking into the morass of moral collapse. Ferree, in noting that women have generally been relational, says:

> Even the edgier *Fifty Shades of Grey* material, which contains stark depictions of BDSM (bondage, dominance, and sadomasochism) is set within an unfolding relationship story. As surprising

as it may sound, *Fifty Shades* is considered vanilla "mommy porn" by the younger generation.[15]

No doubt much of what is watched by Christians includes men and woman performing oral and anal sex on each other (sodomy), which is generally viewed as tamer than what is referred to as BDSM. Pornographic images fix themselves in the brain, evoke the desire for acting out the pornography, and lead to an acceptance of oral sex as a natural form of sexual enjoyment. Then, as lust increases, anal sex and even some of the other sexual practices of homosexuals are tried. Furthermore, as heterosexual Christians engage in the same sexual practices as homosexuals they become more open to other sexual practices devised by those who are not able to perform coital sex with their chosen like-sex partners.

Trends among Christians Regarding Acceptance of Homosexuality

Under the headline "Most U.S. Christian groups grow more accepting of homosexuality," the Pew Research Center reports:

> Amid a changing religious landscape that has seen a declining percentage of Americans who identify as Christian, a majority of U.S. Christians (54%) now say that homosexuality should be accepted, rather than discouraged, by society.

They further say that:

> ... the Christian figure has increased by 10 percentage points since we conducted a similar study in 2007. It reflects a growing acceptance of

homosexuality among all Americans – from 50% to 62% – during the same period.[16]

Another Pew Research Center report, titled "Where Christian churches, other religions stand on gay marriage," concludes:

> Overall, a solid majority of white mainline Protestants (62%) now favor allowing gays and lesbians to wed, with just 33% opposed, according to a 2015 Pew Research Center survey. A similar share (63%) say there is "no conflict" between their religious beliefs and homosexuality.[17]

A sociologist at the University of Texas used the data from the *Relationship in America* survey that interviewed 15,738 Americans, ages 18-60 in 2014 and found that "Churchgoing Christians who support same-sex marriage look very much like the country as a whole," with regard to agreeing with the following statements:

> Viewing pornography is OK.

> Premarital cohabitation is good.

> No-strings-attached sex is OK.

> I support abortion rights.[18]

The more liberal churches generally support homosexual sexual practices between same-sex couples and hetero-sex couples.[19] In fact, they are not really concerned much about what the Bible says on these things and, instead, tend towards mercy without truth when it comes to sexual choices, sexual practices, or sexual identification. On the other hand, the more conservative churches, which take the Bible literally and seriously, are more apt to turn to the Bible to see what God has said concerning personal conduct. They look to God's truth, with the understanding that God is merciful to all sinners who repent and that the greatest mercy is presenting God's truth that can save a person from having to experience His wrath. Nevertheless, what we are seeing is that many of the more conservative churches are losing their hold on biblical truth and personal morality as many individual members are participating in both oral and anal sex as well as other variations with accompanying toys and videos.

Christian Sex Manuals

Currently there are numerous Christian sex manuals describing the intimate details of marital sex. Fifty years ago such Christian sex manuals did not exist and the current-day detailed descriptions were never seen in Christian books. Certainly no one was advocating oral and/or anal sex. We have selected a few contemporary Christian sex manuals to reveal the history and development of these sex manuals and to show that there has been a progression from the first inclusion of oral sex and the later recommendation for anal sex by Christian authors.

The Act of Marriage: The Beauty of Sexual Love by Tim and Beverly Lahaye in 1976. was a ground-breaking book about sex that was written for Christians.[20] Counting the subsequent editions, there have been "over 25 million copies sold since its release."[21] Prior to writing the book, the LaHayes conducted a survey of Christians. They say: "Twenty-three hundred couples volunteered to take the survey, but the final number that were completed and returned totaled 3,377—1,705 women and 1,672 men."[22] The LaHayes compared their results with the results of a *Redbook* magazine survey of 100,000 women from the general population and concluded that the *Redbook* "findings stood in basic agreement with our own."[23]

While the LaHayes do not favor anal intercourse, they say, "The Bible is completely silent" on the practice of oral sex. They further say:

> We do not personally recommend or advocate it [oral sex], but we have no biblical grounds for forbidding it between two married people who mutually enjoy it. We do not think, moreover, that it should be used as a substitute for coitus; if it has a place in marriage, we would suggest it be limited to foreplay.[24]

In their updated edition of *The Act of Marriage* (2000) titled *The Act of Marriage after 40: Making Love for Life*, the LaHayes report that they "conducted a comprehensive, seventy-one question survey of 800 Christian couples on our mailing list."[25] In their latest survey they continue to "not favor anal intercourse" but regarding oral sex, they say:

> Generally speaking, a little more than half of the couples engage in oral sex regularly or periodically—predominantly the latter. **You won't find a "thou shalt" or a "thou shalt not" in Scripture; the Bible is completely silent on this subject.** When we wrote *The Act of Marriage* [1976 edition], we surveyed Christian doctors regarding their opinions: 73 percent felt it was acceptable for a Christian couple as long as both

partners enjoyed it. To our utter amazement, 77 percent of the ministers felt oral sex was acceptable…. Therefore we do not personally recommend or advocate oral sex, but we see no biblical grounds to preclude two married people from enjoying the practice, if they mutually agree that this is something they want to incorporate into their lovemaking, with the *proviso* that it not be used as a substitute for coitus.[26] (Bold added.)

Many books on marriage written for Christians by popular and highly respected Christians endorse and attempt to biblically justify oral sex. For example, Kevin Leman, in his book *Sheet Music: The Secrets of Sexual Intimacy in Marriage* (2003, 2008),[27] warns against anal sex,[28] but recommends oral sex in marriage.[29] He primes his readers in Chapter 5 by detailing numerous various sexual coital positions. [30] Then two chapters later he introduces what he calls "Oral Delights" and gives detailed directions on the use of lips, tongue, and mouth for how a wife can best orally pleasure her husband and how a husband can best orally pleasure his wife.[31] Leman has received 4.7 out of 5 stars from 643 Amazon customer reviews.[32] The cover of Leman's book indicates that Leman is a "*New York Times* best-selling author" and claims "More than ¼ million satisfied couples." Because of the plethora of reviews of *Sheet Music*, no doubt written by Christians, we could not read all of them, but we did read the ones on the "critical" list. **We found only one reviewer, out of the many critical reviews we read, who biblically questioned the support for oral sex or disputed the graphic details of how best to perform oral sex in Leman's book.**

Real Marriage

The popularity of Mark and Grace Driscoll's book *Real Marriage: The Truth About Sex, Friendship, and Life Together* (2012) is a clear demonstration of how far the sexual revolution has brought Christians into the world. In spite of the controversial plan used to boost the book's sales to make *The New York Times* best-seller list, it is a very popular book among Christians.[33]

Recognizing that sexual practices between Christian couples have changed dramatically over the years, the Driscolls preface their sections on "Masturbation," "Oral Sex," "Anal Sex," "Menstrual Sex," "Role Playing," and "Sex Toys" with the following warning:

> If you are older, from a highly conservative religious background, live far away from a major city, do not spend much time on the Internet, or do not have cable television, the odds are that you will want to read this chapter while sitting down, with the medics ready on speed dial.[34]

Thus, if you believe in the authority of God's Word and are walking with Him throughout the day and acknowledging His presence while enjoying His gift of coital sex, then the very idea of promoting the practice of sodomy (oral and anal sex) will be shocking to you, because it is an offense against God and His sexual design for mankind.

After describing the sexual climate of Corinth at the time of Paul's letter, the Driscolls put forth one verse by which to examine various sexual practices, including some that have been borrowed from same-sex sexual acts: "All things are lawful unto me, but all things are not expedient: all things are lawful for me, but I will not be brought under the power of any" (1 Cor. 6"12). With this single, out-of-context verse, the Driscolls mistakenly free people to engage in any or all of the previously mentioned sexual activities. Prior to each individual sexual act, they ask three questions: *"Is it lawful?" "Is it helpful?" "Is it enslaving?"* (Italics in original.) **They fail to ask, "Is this God honoring?"**

While all six of the previously mentioned sexual activities are violations of God's design, two of them—oral and anal sex—are among the leading homosexual practices. After describing oral sex and seemingly justifying it by quoting statistics of large numbers of individuals doing it, the Driscolls answer the question *"Is it lawful?"* by saying, " Oral sex is lawful both culturally and biblically."[35] After attempting to justify oral sex with an erroneous interpretation of the Song of Solomon; which we will discuss later, they say, "In summary, oral sex is permissible within the context of marriage. It is certainly not required, but it is permitted."[36]

The Driscolls answer the question *"Is it helpful?"* by saying, "Yes. Many husbands and wives enjoy oral sex." **Evidently "helpful" equals "enjoyable."** Under "helpful" they should have mentioned health problems related to oral sex, which we will discuss later. And, finall , in answer to the question *"Is it enslaving?"* the Driscolls say, "So long as it is part of a couple's sexual life and not the primary sexual act, then it is a **gift being stewarded well**" (bold added).[37] Oral sex was actively practiced among pagan societies. To call it a "gift being stewarded well" reveals how pagan our culture has become and how pagan the church is becoming. Having not bothered to ask if oral sex is God-honoring, they would have no answer.

The Driscolls then move to "Anal Sex" with the same three questions. In answer to "*Is it lawful?*" they say, "Yes, legally and biblically anal sex is permissible for a married couple, as Scripture does not forbid it."[38] After describing what happened in Sodom and Gomorrah, they declare: "The sin of Sodom was not anal sex between husband and wives [sic], but rather homosexual sex between men, which the Bible repeatedly forbids." The Driscolls mistakenly divorce the act of anal sex from the act of sodomy in an effort to purify it for Christians and wrongly conclude: "Therefore, anal sex within marriage is not sodomy, is not inherently sinful, and is permissible."[39] The Driscolls evidently do not know the legal definition of "sodomy," which is: "Sexual activity that involves oral or anal copulation, whether with the same or opposite sex." *The Legal Dictionary* also says:

> In the law, the term *sodomy* refers to anal or oral sex, whether between a man and woman, two women, or two men, and was historically considered to be a criminal act. As recently as the 1960s, all 50 states had laws that made even consensual sodomy illegal, viewing such acts as "crimes against nature," or deviant sexual acts…. Although sodomy laws applied to both hetero- and homosexual activities, enforcement was often specifically ta geted toward homosexuals.[40]

Although this is not a biblical definition per se, it is what has been understood through the centuries before the sexual revolution. Even though the attempted sexual assault on Lot's guests was for same-sex sodomy, the act itself rebels against God's design. Remember, the reason for oral and anal sex is because men do not have a vagina. Therefore homosexual men use the mouth and anus in place of the vagina.

In answer to the question "*Is it helpful?*" the Driscolls begin by saying, "This is a question that requires earnest consideration by a couple." While offering a suggestion about the use of the wife's finger in the husband's anus and issuing a caution about the possibility of the anus becoming torn and infected, they say"

> Some couples choose to use this method to prevent pregnancy. In conjunction with the rhythm method of birth control in which normal penis-vagina intercourse is suspended on a woman's days of fertility, it is possible to use anal sex as an option.[41]

The Dricolls answer "*Is it enslaving?*" with: "If anal sex becomes an obsessive part of the marriage or begins to overtake other forms of marital sex, especially penis-vagina sex, then there may be a problem."[42]

On three pages of the book, under the title "Praise for *Real Marriage*," there are ten written endorsements for the book, which are filled with glowing reports, recommendations, and high praise encouraging readers to obtain the book and profit from its messages. Seven are by pastors, two by seminary faculty members, and one by a couple who are popular Christian authors.

Forbes magazine identifi s Driscoll as "one of the nation's most prominent and celebrated pastors."[43] Since this book was written by such a well-known pastor and his wife describing *Real Marriage* for Christians, we wondered about the reader responses on Amazon.com. Out of almost 600 reviews, the Dricolls received a score of 4.2 out of 5 stars! We did not read all of the almost 600 reviews, but we did read a number of them. **Not one criticized the Driscolls' recommendations on sexual practices for being contrary to God's design for marriage.**

Before summarizing the progression of oral and anal sex in the church, we comment on one of the best-known classics for Christians on sex. Ed Wheat, MD, and Gaye Wheat's book *Intended for Pleasure: Sex Technique and Sexual Fulfillment in Christian Marriage* was first published in 1977, just one year after the LaHayes' book. Since its original printing there have been "More than 1 Million Copies Sold."[44] The Wheats say nothing about anal sex, but do not express direct opposition to oral sex. In the answer to one question about oral sex, they do recommend that a couple "provide a maximum of physical pleasure for both through regular intercourse." They do recommend "experiencing the unity and oneness that God has designed for their human bodies in basic sexual intercourse."[45] We agree! **According to God's design, which is coital intercourse, and not man's devices, such as oral and anal sex (sodomy).** Christians who are practicing and/or promoting oral and anal sex are actually cooperating with the homosexual revisionist view of Scripture.

Note the progression and expansion of the sexual lasciviousness among Christians. The LaHayes, in their *Act of Marriage* (1976), while opposed to anal sex and "do not recommend or advocate" oral sex, could give "no biblical grounds for forbidding it."[46] Years later (2003, 2008), Kevin Leman opposes anal sex, but highly recommends oral sex and gives detailed instructions on how, in marriage, a wife can best do it to satisfy her husband and how a husband can best do it to satisfy his wife. Not too many years later (2012) the Driscolls, through their faulty biblical reasoning and by erroneously interpreting the Song of Solomon, recommend and justify both oral and anal sex, as well as other variant sexual practices for married couples. Christians have thus been taken in by the sexual revolution and have written books to inform other Christians about the possibilities of heterosexually engaging in sexual activities that in previous ages would have been considered only homosexual practices.

Argument from Silence

The following are arguments used by many Christians for oral sex, anal sex, or both:

Tim and Beverly Lahaye, in their book *The Act of Marriage after 40: Making Love for Life* say regarding oral sex: "You won't find a 'thou shalt' or a 'thou shalt not' in Scripture; the Bible is **completely silent** on this subject"[47] (bold added).

Kevin Leman, in his book *Sheet Music: The Secrets of Sexual Intimacy in Marriage*, says, "In fact, the Bible is **silent** on whether marital oral sex is immoral—which says to most Bible scholars that it must be okay"[48] (bold added).

Mark and Grace Driscoll, in their book *Real Marriage: The Truth about Sex, Friendship, and Life Together*, say: "Yes, legally and biblically anal sex is permissible for a married couple, as Scripture **does not forbid it**"[49] (bold added).

The argument from silence is found on many popular websites, media, books, and teaching materials throughout Christendom. For example, Focus on the Family, which is "carried daily on 2,000 radio outlets in the United States and has become one of today's most recognized Christian radio programs,"[50] says on their website under the heading "Oral and Anal Sex: Biblical Guidelines for Intimacy in Marriage":

> The Bible **never addresses the question** of oral sex in marriage, and for this reason it's our opinion that this issue must be left to a couple's own judgement.... **Something similar might be said with regard to anal sex**, but it is crucial to add that we have special concerns about this practice.[51] (Bold added.)

The above are all logical fallacies known as *argumentum ex silentio* or "argument from silence." When the argument from silence is used there must be substantial reasons for doing so. However, to be consistent, **once the argument from silence is used, it needs to be applied in all similar case**s. In contrast, from their above oral sex quote, the LaHayes say, "There is one sexual act that we do not favor: anal intercourse."[52] Also, in contrast to the above oral sex quote from Kevin Leman, he says about anal sex, "It's best to leave this practice alone.... It's kinky, and I believe it's wrong."[53] Out of the three books, only the Driscolls are consistent by recommending both oral and anal sex, although they are in gross biblical error for doing so.

In the above Focus on the Family example, it is admitted by them that the argument from silence applies to both oral and anal sex. They are consistent when they say that the Bible never addresses either oral or anal sex, but Focus on the Family only has "special concerns about" anal sex.

The LaHayes and Leman are consistently inconsistent in using an argument from silence regarding oral sex while failing to apply the silence argument to anal sex. However, Focus on the Family is consistently consistent by applying the argument of silence to both oral and anal sex, but they are in violation of Scripture for doing so. Also, there are other homosexual sexual practices that could be rationalized by the argument from silence, all of which they would probably be against.

The LaHayes, Leman, and the Driscolls apparently do not realize that the argument from silence can be turned around to say that, since God did not name oral or anal sex in His Word, He, therefore, by not naming these sexual practices has not given his permission for either to be done by believers. To reverse the argument from silence in its pro-oral-pro-anal-use, we could say that, **because the area of human sexuality is so important to God and an essential ingredient in His creative sexual design, if He had wanted oral and anal sex to be enjoyed by His people, He would have said so in Scripture.**

Pastor John Piper, in his openness to oral sex, says: "I don't think oral sex is explicitly prohibited in any biblical command."[54] Neither are the various other unclean, unhealthy, and disgusting sexual behaviors of homosexuals "explicitly prohibited in any biblical command"! This is just another variation of the argument from silence.

In contrast to that, we ask, "Is it explicitly included in the Bible?" The answer is "no." Please note that a woman's breasts are included in Proverbs 5:19, "let her breasts satisfy thee at all times; and be thou ravished always with her love." The Song of Solomon 7:7-8 says:

> How fair and how pleasant art thou, O love, for delights! This thy stature is like to a palm tree, and thy breasts to clusters of grapes. I said, I will go up to the palm tree, I will take hold of the boughs thereof: now also thy breasts shall be as clusters of the vine, and the smell of thy nose like apples.

Although a woman's breasts are directly named and included as part and parcel of sexual pleasure, oral sex is neither named, nor included, but only inferred and imposed on the text by those, influenced by the sexual revolution, who see the Song of Solomon in that new way in contrast to the traditional orthodox way, as we describe in Chapter 6.

A woman's breasts are part of the marriage relationship to be enjoyed by both the husband and wife, but Satan uses the desirable qualities of a woman's breasts to tempt men to lust after other women. Such visual temptations are everywhere, particularly in the media's public promotion of sexual uncleanness and fornication. The exposing of women's breasts in the variety of public venues is often the doorway into pornography for men. This God-given goodness, created for nurture and marital intimacy, is corrupted by the world, lusted after in the flesh, and orchestrated by the devil

Kissing is also included in Scripture. There are over 70 references in the Bible to kiss, kissed, and kisses that reveal a variety of circumstances and participants. The Song of Solomon includes two references to kissing: "Let him kiss me with the kisses of his mouth: for thy love is better than wine" (Song 1:2) and "When I should find thee without, I would kiss thee" (Song 8:1). Because of the context, we conclude that these are intimate kisses enjoyed by both the man and the woman and are an example of intimacy a husband and wife can enjoy.

We define earlier in Chapter 2 the "activist" as "an especially active, vigorous advocate of a cause" and a "revisionist," as one who "vigorously advocate[s]" for "revision of an accepted usually long-standing…doctrine." We indicate that many homosexual activists are revisionists because they reinterpret the orthodox biblical understanding of sodomy. **We now say that those Christians, including the LaHayes, Leman, the Driscolls, Focus on the Family, Piper, and many others, who use the argument from silence to support oral and/or anal sex, are also activists who are also revisionists of the orthodox biblical understanding of God's design for human sexuality as we describe in Chapter 1.**

Lovers of Pleasure More than Lovers of God

One would think that Christians would shun those activities that go against God's design for sexual intimacy, but the bold truth is that many Christians have been reading and following such sex books in their own secret places with a misunderstanding of "the marriage bed." Perhaps they assume that as long as sexual activities are performed within a marital union of husband and wife anything goes—even watching pornography together and trying out pornographic activities. Christians are embracing the world and being influenced by a very sexually promiscuous culture. In addition, more and more websites and books are being aimed at Christians to help them expand their sexual pleasure possibilities, all within a so-called Christian framework.

As America has followed the sexual revolution and numerous forms of the fleshly wisdom of men that God condemns, one finds that whatever seems good to each individual is the substance of that person's morality. Americans are simply doing what they think is right in their own eyes, just as Israel did during a bleak time of rebellion: "In those days there was no king in Israel: every man did that which was right in his own eyes" (Judges 17:6; 21:26). Just as Israel was not honoring God, so with America. Pleasure and self-satisfaction often take precedence over any thought of God, who created and sustains human life. One can see how the progression of Romans 1:18-32 is happening in the world as relativistic morality and open sexuality are on the increase.

Our concern is with Christians who are following the ways of the world. The apostle Paul pleads with Christians:

> This I say therefore, and testify in the Lord, that ye henceforth walk not as other Gentiles walk, in the vanity of their mind, Having the understanding darkened, being alienated from the life of God through the ignorance that is in them, because of the blindness of their heart: Who being **past feel-**

**ing have given themselves over unto lascivi-
ousness, to work all uncleanness** with greediness. (Eph. 4:17-19, bold added.)

In His high-priestly prayer, Jesus prayed thus to the
Father:

> I have given them thy word; and the world hath
> hated them, because **they are not of the world,
> even as I am not of the world**. I pray not that
> thou shouldest take them out of the world, but
> that thou shouldest keep them from the evil. **They
> are not of the world, even as I am not of the
> world**. Sanctify them through thy truth: thy word
> is truth. As thou hast sent me into the world, even
> so have I also sent them into the world. And for
> their sakes I sanctify myself, that they also might
> be sanctified through the truth. Neither pray I for
> these alone, but for them also which shall believe
> on me through their word. (John 17:14-20, bold
> added).

Christians are to be "not of the world" even as Jesus
was "not of the world." Nevertheless we are seeing a
dramatic shift in the church as more and more people
who identify as Christians are losing their hold on Christ
and the Word of God. Many are adjusting their morality to fit in with the world as they absorb more from the
media than they may realize. Many have looked to the
world for dealing with the issues of life instead of turning to the Lord and His Word. In doing so, they have
followed the ways of the flesh.

**Each step of compromise with the ways of the
world, the flesh, and the devil leads away from God**

and the clear truth of His Word. As a result, many leaders in the church have been reconsidering what the Bible says about human sexuality and homosexuality and many have been revising their understanding of the Bible to fit in with a full acceptance of sodomy and the homosexual lifestyle.

6

The Song of Solomon

Over the years various scholars have disagreed over the title of the Song, whether to call it "The Song of Solomon," "Canticles," or "The Song of Songs." In this chapter we will refer to it as the "Song." The Song weaves the intricacies of the relationship between one man and one woman designed by God. How are a man and woman drawn together to form one being? The Song poignantly prompts the sensations of desire and admiration. But to understand the Song, we must begin at the beginning of God's creation where He reveals the profound mystery of the union of two different personalities with differing physical and emotional characteristics, flawlessly designed to complement and enhance each other in the perfection of marriage before it was marred by sin.

The Song is truly the Song of Songs in its poetic construction and its sexual purity. The Song extols the beauty of the intimate oneness of relationship between the man and the woman, as God created sexual love in all its beauty, passion, and fruitfulness. However, because of sin, this diamond centerpiece of relationship with all its facets has been misunderstood, abused, and even covered over with the fig leaves of human fear. The Song is the drama of a love relationship between a man and woman where desire for each other and passions are kept within the framework of fidelity and within the context of God's perfect love in creation. The love song extends far deeper than physical intimacy alone. Although the yearnings are expressed in physical terms appealing to the five senses, the deep longing is for one another's company—to be with each other in heart, soul, mind, and body.

J. Paul Tanner, who specializes in Hebrew and Old Testament Studies, says:

> Probably no other book in all the Bible has given rise to such a plethora of interpretations as the Song of Songs. Saadia, a medieval Jewish commentator said the Song of Songs is like a book for which the key has been lost.[1]

Tanner names and discusses over a dozen different major interpretations of the Song. In the numerous commentaries, books, and articles, we read a variety of interpretations from the allegorical to the literal to the dream to the contemporary exotic.

Most commentaries on the Song express the great difficulty in interpreting it, particularly in its details. For instance, William McDonald declares, "This song, also called Canticles, is generally considered the hardest book in the Bible to *understand*" (italics his).[2] Another Bible scholar considered the Song to be "the most obscure book in the Old Testament."[3] In puzzling over how one might interpret the Song, MacDonald says:

> Here the imagination of readers throughout the ages has had a field day. While certain Jews and Christians have prudishly avoided the book as "sensual," some of the most devout saints throughout history have reveled in its pages.[4]

The Bible is all about relationship: God's love for the people He created as relational beings and their love for one another. Over the years many Bible scholars interpreted the Song exclusively as a poetic expression of the love bond between God and His people. Other passages in Scripture echo this graphic illustration of God's ultimate goal of a heavenly marriage between Himself and His people (e.g., Eph. 5:22-33; Rev. 19:9). Jews believed that the Song extolled the love relationship between Jehovah and His chosen people. Rather than being interpreted literally, the Song was accepted as allegory with the human love expressions being attributed to God and Israel. Bible scholar Andrew Fausset reports:

> The Jews compared Proverbs to the outer court of Solomon's temple, Ecclesiastes to the holy place, and Canticles to the holy of holies. Understood allegorically, the Song is cleared of all difficult . "Shulamite" (So 6:13), the bride, is thus an appropriate name, *Daughter of Peace* being the feminine of Solomon, equivalent to the *Prince of Peace.*[5]

For centuries Christian Bible scholars interpreted the Song allegorically as a picture of the love relationship between Christ and His church. For instance, Matthew Henry in his commentary says:

> It is a song, an *Epithalamium*, or nuptial song, wherein, by the expressions of love between a bridegroom and his bride, are set forth and illustrated the mutual affections that pass between God and a distinguished remnant of mankind. It is a pastoral; the bride and bridegroom, for the more lively representation of humility and innocence, are brought in as a shepherd and his shepherdess…. This song might easily be taken in a spiritual sense by the Jewish church, for whose use it was first composed, and was so taken, as appears by the Chaldee-Paraphrase and the most ancient Jewish expositors. God betrothed the people of Israel to himself; he entered into covenant with them, and it was a marriage-covenant…. It may more easily be taken in a spiritual sense by the Christian church, because the condescensions and communications of divine love appear more rich and free under the gospel than they did under the law, and the communion between heaven and earth more familiar. God sometimes spoke of himself as the husband of the Jewish church (Isa. 64:5, Hos. 2:16, 19), and rejoiced in it as his bride, Isa. 62:4, 5. But more frequently is Christ represented as the bridegroom of his church (Mt. 25:1; Rom. 7:4; 2 Co. 11:2; Eph. 5:32), and the church as the bride, the Lamb's wife, Rev. 19:7; 21:2, 9. Pursuant to this metaphor Christ and the church in general, Christ and particular believers,

are here discoursing with abundance of mutual esteem and endearment.[6]

More recent commentators recognize the historical use of allegory in bringing understanding to the Song, but they deal with the Song as a poem about romantic or sexual love. Even here there is much variety as some see the Song as a collection of songs and others see it as one Song with the use of repetition and refrains. Some identify the two lovers as Solomon and the Shulamite with or without a story line, while others contend that the Shulamite and her shepherd were lovers, that she resisted the temptation to be won by Solomon, and that she was faithful to her shepherd-lover.

In his commentary on the Song, Jack Deere says:

> The purpose of the book is to extol human love and marriage. Though at first this seems strange, on reflection it is not surprising for God to have included in the biblical canon a book endorsing the beauty and purity of marital love. God created man and woman (Gen. 1:27; 2:20–23) and established and sanctioned marriage (Gen. 2:24). Since the world views sex so sordidly and perverts and exploits it so persistently and since so many marriages are crumbling because of lack of love, commitment, and devotion, it is advantageous to have a book in the Bible that gives God's endorsement of marital love as wholesome and pure.[7]

Nevertheless, during the years following the sexual revolution in this country, the Song has been used to justify impure sexual practices outside God's sexual design.

Verses have been misinterpreted to accommodate oral sex—not only to make it acceptable, but even to make it a marital requirement.[8]

Transmogrifying the Song

Interpretations of the Song that include oral sex, which is a homosexual sex-act substitute for coital sex, are of recent vintage. They have come as a result of the 20th Century sexual revolution and can only be found by one who allows his/her own lust to see what is clearly not there. Although Solomon disobeyed God by marrying many women and having a harem full of concubines, the Song is attributed to him, but not by all commentators. Nevertheless, because it was inspired by the Holy Spirit, the Song shows forth the depth of love between a man and woman, expressed in physical desire **according to God's sexual design**. The Song would not portray this one paradigm of sexual love by inferring or suggesting by double entendre any sexual activities outside His perfect sexual design.

In reading and re-reading the Song many times and perusing plenty of books, commentaries and websites, we decided that, for the purpose of this book, we would only deal with Song 2:3 and 4:16-5:1, since these are the verses that are being misused to promote oral sex. Song 2:3 reads: "As the apple tree among the trees of the wood, so is my beloved among the sons. I sat down under his shadow with great delight, and his fruit was sweet to my taste." For example, Mark and Grace Driscoll claim that Song 2:3 "speaks of oral sex in a positive and poetic fashion." They then quote Joseph Dillow's book *Solomon on Sex*: "In extra biblical literature, fruit is sometimes equated with the male genitals or with semen, so it is possible that here we have a faint and delicate reference to an oral genital caress."[9]

The claim that the expression "his fruit was sweet to my taste" refers to a woman performing oral sex (fellatio) on her lover would be to exalt fornication as well as uncleanness, since the wedding does not occur until chapter 3 of the Song. The obvious retort is that the woman is fantasizing or dreaming that she is performing oral sex on her lover. But, desirously imagining performing oral sex would be sinful, as Jesus warned about lustful thinking (Matt. 5:28). Moreover, whether the woman is dreaming or fantasizing, the very inclusion of oral sex as a positive sexual expression in the Bible would be a corruption—an abomination!

A second place where the Dricolls interpret the Song with their own personal acceptance and public promotion of oral sex is in Chapter 4:16-5:1:

> Awake, O north wind; and come, thou south; blow upon my garden, that the spices thereof may flow out. Let my beloved come into his garden, and eat his pleasant fruits. I am come into my garden, my sister, my spouse: I have gathered my myrrh with my spice; I have eaten my honeycomb with my honey; I have drunk my wine with my milk: eat, O friends; drink, yea, drink abundantly, O beloved.

The Driscolls continue their interpretation of the Song 4:16-5:1 and say that "her moist vagina is likened to a fresh spring." They interpret this passage as the woman inviting the "man to perform oral sex (cunnilingus) on her." And although there is no mention of God in the Song, the Driscolls have Him right there to encourage the act of oral sex by attributing the words in Song 5:1 to God, "Eat, friends, and drink; drink your fill of love" (NIV).[10]

Such interpretations do not come from an understanding of the context of the whole Bible, particularly creation, but are, instead, imposed on the text from one's own imagination. Without the whole counsel of God, one can find all sorts of ideas totally unrelated to what God would ever say. Such an interpretation does not rely on sound rules of hermeneutics, but rather on one's own personal sexual preferences and practices. How often one might be tempted to interpret Scripture to say that what one is doing is of God. Indeed that is what the homosexual activist revisionists do, and that is what the Driscolls and others who put oral sex into the Song are doing: Revise the Word to justify what they choose to do.

There are two important requirements for properly interpreting the Song: a thorough knowledge of Hebrew and hermeneutics, including an understanding of poetic expressions and an extensive knowledge of the cultural context of the Song. With this in mind, we read what a number of scholars with the necessary background had to say about the Song and particularly about Song 2:3 and 4:16-5:1. There are two arguable conclusions we came to: arguable because we could not read all the available scholarly writings. First, although there were differences in their interpretations of the Song, no scholar interpreted the above verses from the Song as having anything to do with fellatio or cunnilingus. We searched commentaries of knowledgeable individuals prior to the sexual revolution and found no such interpretations of fellatio and cunnilingus as put forth by those who audaciously author books and preach about sex for Christians.

Our second arguable conclusion is that the oral sex interpretation reveals a gender bias in that we found no female scholar, although not in agreement with each other, who interpreted the above Song verses as involving oral sex! We suspect that those Christians who interpret oral sex in the Song are all men who are practicing it in their marriages. That seems reasonable because men interpret Song 2:3 as the woman performing oral sex on the man and they interpret Song 4:16-5:1 as the man orally stimulating the woman. To paraphrase an old adage: One sees oral sex not as it is in the Song, but as it is in the eyes of one who is already doing it.

As a prime example of how prolifically the Song is misinterpreted and misused, we refer to an article we wrote on the counseling of Dr. Heath Lambert, who is probably one of the best-known and highly respected leaders of the biblical counseling movement in the world. Lambert's credits include the following:

> Dr. Heath Lambert is the Executive Director at the Association of Certified Biblical Counselors. ACBC is the largest biblical counseling organization in the world with counseling training centers and certified counselors in 29 countries

> Dr. Lambert also serves as the Associate Pastor and Executive Pastor for Discipleship and Family Life at First Baptist Church in Jacksonville, FL.

Dr. Lambert is a faculty member at The Southern Baptist Theological Seminary and their undergraduate institution, Boyce College, where he has taught since 2006.[11]

Lambert, in a three-part DVD, produced and promoted by the Institute for Biblical Counseling and Discipleship (IBCD), demonstrates (by play-acting) how to counsel a man "Jeremy," who has a "long-standing enslavement to pornography." We excerpt from the article:

This third play-acted session then deals with the subject of "Crystal's" ["Jeremy's" wife] upcoming post-birth condition, which was said to make her unavailable for sexual intercourse for six weeks, and the impact that may have on "Jeremy's" perceived dire necessity for sex possibly precipitating a return to pornography. Lambert says, "As far as sexual intimacy is concerned, why don't you look at Song of Solomon, Chapter 2." Lambert then reads verses 3-7 from the *English Standard Version* (*ESV*):

> As an apple tree among the trees of the forest, so is my beloved among the young men.
>
> With great delight I sat in his shadow, and his fruit was sweet to my taste.
>
> He brought me to the banqueting house, and his banner over me was love.
>
> Sustain me with raisins; refresh me with apples, for I am sick with love.
>
> His left hand is under my head, and his right hand embraces me!

> I adjure you, O daughters of Jerusalem, by the
> gazelles or the does of the field, that you not stir
> up or awaken love until it pleases.

After reading the Song of Solomon, Lambert explains:

> What the woman is saying here is that—using
> very poetic imagery—she's saying that in their
> intimate relationship there was an entire banquet
> of things that they were doing together. And she
> is saying, "I enjoyed all of them. I enjoy being
> with my husband sexually in **all the ways** that
> you can be." So I think this is a passage of the
> Bible that teaches us poetically that there's **all
> kinds of things** that married couples can do to
> enjoy one another in the context of sexual inti-
> macy. (Bold added.)

Lambert later says:

> This is a picture of a woman who is **loving the
> buffet of sexuality** with her husband and in the
> context of that she delights to be embraced by
> him. (Bold added.)

The meaning of "all the ways" as in "I enjoy being
with my husband sexually in all the ways that you can be"
is "in every way." The meaning of "all kinds of things,"
as in "there's all kinds of things that married couples can
do to enjoy one another in the context of sexual intimacy," is "an unlimited number of things." The word *buffet*,
as in "loving the buffet of sexuality" means a tempting
variety of sexuality. **In no way is it possible to infer or
imagine that the woman in Song of Solomon would be
interested in or expecting pornographically inspired**

sex, but Lambert fails to explain this to "Jeremy" and "Crystal"! This is a serious omission as Lambert euphemistically describes the possibilities:

> You don't have to have sexual intercourse in order to be able to be sexually fulfilled during this season of your marriage.

A little later Lambert explains:

> And so, this can be a time that is really sweet for both of you. She's going to be—she's going to have some limitations on her physical body as to **how she can serve you in that way—but she can still serve you**. But you ["Jeremy"] are going to be **unlimited** in your ability to draw near to her to embrace her, to rub her arm, to rub her hair until she falls asleep. (Bold added.)

The word *unlimited*, as in "But you ["Jeremy"] are going to be unlimited," simply means that there will be no limit to "Jeremy's" "ability to draw near to her." Though all of the above seems well-intentioned, it is ill advised and is an egregious error and sets an unbiblical example for counselors to follow, which any hardcore porn user can capitalize on.

Although Lambert did not explicitly use the words "oral sex," the implication is clearly there, especially for anyone who has feasted on porn and especially with the words: **"she can still serve you"** and **"you are going to be unlimited."** "Unlimited" would no doubt include anal sex to "Jeremy," a hardcore porn user. Remember, these play-acted sessions occurred about 8 years after the Driscolls' book and over 30 years after Dillow's book.

One wonders how many biblical counselors and pastors have been sanctifying oral sex to married couples under their counsel and care. In response to the popularity of sermons recommending sexual exploits at the expense of the Song, Dr. John MacArthur titled a series of four excellent articles "The Rape of Solomon's Song," critical of Mark Driscoll's teachings. MacArthur began his first article with these words: "Apparently the shortest route to *relevance* in church ministry right now is for the pastor to talk about sex in garishly explicit terms during the Sunday morning service" (emphasis his).[12] Although there are questions about the details of the Song, oral sex could not be in it, because the rest of the Bible calls sodomy "abomination."

Reclaiming the Song

We grieve over the fact that Christian leaders have used the Song to promote lustful sexual behavior that is contrary to God's design. We further grieve over having to place details of this corruption before the body of Christ. However, such exposure and warning are necessary in these days of sexual promiscuity and impurity within the church. Believers need to wrest the Song away from such lustful corruptions, declare its devotion to God's design, and celebrate its purity and power: purity in procreation and power in faithfulness. Consider God's primary purpose in His sexual design: Procreation! Fruitfulness! Neither fellatio nor cunnilingus can produce new life; in fact, they interfere as substitutes for life-producing coital sex. Therefore they have no place in this beautiful Song that celebrates life, love, fruitfulness, and abundant provision. There is no hint of uncleanness or fornication within its stanzas. Instead, the imagery is much about the fruitfulness and faithfulness of one-flesh. The garden imagery recalls the Garden of Eden in its lush provision, pleasure, and purity. The Song exemplifies human love within the chasteness of court-ship and marriage. The Song sings of the love of one man and one woman being drawn together into one flesh.

Imagery is used in poetry to convey ideas and feel-ings through sensory impressions. Thus images of sight, sound, taste, smell, and touch in the Song convey intense love and devotion to one another as well as the hope of abundant provision, procreation, and pleasure. These images also work for those who interpret the Song as the relationship of God to his wife, Israel, and to Christ and His bride, the church. In fact, one can appreciate and apply the Song according to both interpretations. Thus, "His banner over me was love" (Song 2:4) can remind us of God's faithful love and a husband's love and care for his wife.

In Song 7:2-3, the images of the woman's navel being like a "round goblet" full of liquor, her belly being like a "heap of wheat set about with lilies," and her breasts "like two young roes" not only speak of her physical per-fection, but her ability to conceive, carry and nourish an infant in her womb, and continue to nourish the young child with her breasts. Applying the verses spiritually would be to see God's initial giving of life and provid-ing for His people both physically and spiritually. The placement of the Song right near the middle of the Bible should remind all of us of the fact that it must be read within the context of all of Scripture, not as an isolated piece of poetry. **As one reads the Song and applies it** in marriage or in relationship to Christ, one must remember the beginning of the story: "God created...."

7

Dangers and Diseases of Sodomy

The homosexual sexual violations of God's design for sexuality of one man and one woman in a committed relationship of marriage leads to a whole litany of health hazards—some leading to disablement and even death. Those Christians who are contaminating the marriage bed by practicing the homosexual acts of oral and/or anal sex are, first and foremost, violating God's sacred sexual design and, secondly, opening their bodies to the possibility of damage that is downright dangerous if not outright lethal.

Under the section heading "Homosexuals Die Young," The Family Research Institute report titled "Medical Consequences of What Homosexuals Do" says:

> Smokers and drug addicts don't live as long as non-smokers or non-addicts, so we consider smoking and narcotics abuse harmful. The typical lifespan of homosexuals suggests that their

activities are more destructive than smoking and about as dangerous as drugs.[1]

It would be helpful if such a study could be done of heterosexuals who practice oral and/or anal sex and their longevity.

O. R. Adams, in his book *As We Sodomize America: The Homosexual Movement and the Decline of Morality in America*, names over a half a dozen sexual acts, in which homosexuals engage.[2] However, since we are writing to and for Christians, we describe and discuss the health implications only of oral and anal sex, since these are the two sexual acts of homosexuals that many believers are practicing. Most of the other homosexual sexual practices are transparently harmful and potentially life-threatening. The HIV/AIDS pandemic disease is a direct result of homosexual sexual practices. **It's as if God has programmed into mankind the results of same-sex sexual acts being contrary to what he has ordained and that includes oral and anal sex.**

In Part Two of the Special Report *Sexuality and Gender*, mentioned earlier, the researchers conclude: "Compared to the general population, non-heterosexual subpopulations are at an elevated risk for a variety of adverse health and mental health outcomes."[3] An article titled "Survey Finds Excess Health Problems in Lesbians, Gays, and Bisexuals" says, "Gay, lesbian and bisexual individuals reported more health problems than straight men and women, in a large U.S. survey."[4] Dr. Lorraine Day, an internationally acclaimed orthopedic trauma surgeon has said:

As a physician, I know very well that if we abuse our bodies we will get sick and possibly die. There are very serious health consequences to abusive and self-abusive sexual behavior. Gay males as a rule have been abusive to themselves and to their partners to a degree that is incomprehensible within the heterosexual world.[5]

Anal and Oral Sex

We first deal with anal sex because it is probably the most bodily destructive of the two sinful sodomy sex acts done by many Christians. Unlike the justification by some for oral sex, by wrongly interpreting the Song (see Chapter 6), **there is no justification by any scholar we read for anal sex in the entire Bible**. Those who justify it, use the logical error of "argument from silence," which we debunk in Chapter 5. The argument from silence can only be used erroneously and egregiously to justify all the extreme and health hammering sexual acts of homosexuals.

In discussing anal and oral sex, we will be stating what is generally true of husbands and wives, recognizing that there are exceptions. Usually the only reason why wives participate in anal or oral sex is to please their husbands, who are lusting after it. **Regarding anal and oral sex, the husbands are the aggressors.**

Anal Sex

In Chapter Two we define anal sex: "Anal sex or anal intercourse is generally the insertion and thrusting of the erect penis into a person's anus, or anus and rectum for sexual pleasure."[6] We report in Chapter 5 that a 2008 *To-*

day's Christian Woman sex survey revealed that 77% of the women, in reference to anal sex, checked "Have not done at all." Thus the remaining 23% have submitted to anal sex one or more times. Since 2008, the practice of anal sex has increased rapidly. We know that husbands initiate anal sex and their wives yield to please them. Clifford and Joyce Penner say:

> Anal sex is a practice that typically causes conflict between husbands and wives…and tends to be **initiated and desired by men whose interest got sparked by pornography**. Many sexual experts and medical personnel discourage anal sex because of the danger of transmission of infection and tearing of the blood vessels in the rectum.[7] (Bold added.)

Men tend to be more physical, while women tend to be more relational. An article in *Christian Counseling Today* says it very well: "Women's brains are typically more relationally-attuned."[8] In other words, wives are interested in relational intimacy. A wife is typically not interested in anal sex because it is extremely difficult for her to have intimacy with her back towards her husband while his penis is penetrating her anus. After all, turning one's back is an indication of rejection, refusal, or denial. Moreover, it is painful and, for many wives, just plain disgusting. Anal sex for a husband often results from viewing pornography, lusting after it, and then justifying it with erroneous information about how excellent it is and how desirable it is for his wife.

It is known that anal sex is one of the riskiest forms of sexual activity for a number of reasons. First, the wife's vagina has natural lubrication, which her anus lacks. When the husband's penis penetrates the wife's anal area, it can perforate the tissue inside the wife's anus and thereby spread bacteria and viruses throughout the body via the blood. Moreover, if repeated, anal sex can weaken the anal sphincter and thereby make it difficult to hold in the feces and result in anal incontinence.[9] Anal intercourse can also increase the risk of anal cancer.[10] Although the husband is not as vulnerable as the wife, he is in danger of being infected by various viruses and bacteria in the wife's anus.[11]

Oral Sex

In Chapter Two we define oral sex: "Oral sex is when you stimulate your partner's genitals with your mouth, lips or tongue. This could involve sucking or licking their penis (also called fellatio), vagina, vulva or clitoris (cunnilingus)...."[12] In Chapter 5, in response to the question, "Do you and your husband have oral sex?" the 2008 *Today's Christian Woman* sex survey revealed only 17% responded, "Have not done at all." Thus 83% of the couples have done oral sex one or more times. From 2008 to the present, the number of couples who regularly practice oral sex has, according to other surveys, increased so dramatically that the 5% from the *Today's Christian Woman* sex survey who responded, "Did Once," has probably been a substantial part of the dramatic increase.

As with anal sex, the husbands are the initiators of oral sex, and the wives yield in order to please their husbands. Wives are typically not interested in oral sex, but, because they desire intimacy, yield to it. Unlike anal sex, in which a husband's penis and the wife's anus are involved, oral sex is done with the husband's penis in the wife's mouth or the husband's mouth, tongue, and/or lips used on his wife' clitoris or vagina. The husband's penis has two purposes: sexual intercourse and urination. Therefore, pathogens in the urine flowing thorough the penis can enter the wife's mouth. **Although people have believed that urine is sterile, current research is revealing that it is definitely not steril** .[13]

An infectious diseases journal reports: "Oral sex can transmit oral, respiratory, and genital pathogens. Oral health has a direct impact on the transmission of infection; a cut in your mouth, bleeding gums, lip sores or broken skin increases chances of infection."[14] It is now reported that oral sex can "give people human papilloma virus (HPV) in the throat area," and thereby cause cancer.[15] Regarding oral sex, the National Health Service of the United Kingdom (NHS, UK) says: "It is one of the ways that sexually transmitted infections (STIs) are most frequently passed on." And this concern is not only for people practicing fornication, as the NHS, UK says, **"You can catch an STI if you have just one sexual partner**... STIs that are commonly caught through oral sex are: gonorrhea, genital herpes, syphilis" (bold added).[16]

Worldwide Pandemic

The Centers for Disease Control and Prevention (CDC) say: "HPV is a very common virus; nearly 80 million people—about one in four—are currently infected in the United States."[17] In urging individuals to be vaccinated, the CDC says: "Every year in the United States, 31,000 women and men are diagnosed with a cancer caused by HPV infection. Most of these cancers could be prevented by HPV vaccination."[18] The CDC also reports that sexually transmitted diseases (STDs) are at an "Unprecedented High in the U.S." and that "Chlamydia, gonorrhea and syphilis are the three most commonly reported conditions in the nation and have reached a record high level."[19] The title of an article in *Scientific American* sends a further alarm: "Gonorrhea May Become Resistant to All Antibiotics Sooner than Anticipated."[20]

Another report says that the CDC "estimates that about 19 million new cases of STIs occur each year."[21] Keep in mind, that gonorrhea, as well as HPV virus and syphilis, can be transmitted through oral sex. Viruses and bacteria are all involved in all of the STDs. Although all forms of sexual activity can be avenues for virus and bacteria transmission, oral and anal forms of sex are very vulnerable entryways for STDs to enter and infect the body. Indeed the sexual revolution is bearing its fruit of disease and death, with the CDC recommending that children as young as 11 and 12 years of age be vaccinated for HPV.[22]

Sexually transmitted diseases (STDs) have been around the world for many centuries and are the clear result of fornication. God designed sex to be enjoyed between one man and one woman in a committed relationship, but, as the years of sin accumulated since Eve's first bite, so have the diseases and the numbers of people afflicted. A primary safeguard against such diseases is monogamy: one man and one woman in a faithful, ongoing relationship of marriage. Nevertheless because of the carnal nature of mankind, such a simple solution is not acceptable to many. Therefore the choice is for cures and condoms rather than God's design.

Nineteen-eighty-one was the beginning of the world-wide HIV/AIDS (human immunodeficiency virus/acquired immunodeficiency syndrome) epidemic. During 2016 there were "36.7 million people living with HIV/AIDS Worldwide." During the same year "1.0 million people died of HIV-related illnesses worldwide."[23] The two most practiced sex acts of homosexuals are oral and anal sex (sodomy). **When the HIV/AIDS pandemic occurred, the original main route of the transmission of HIV/AIDS was oral and anal sex by homosexuals.**

A great alarm went out when HIV/AIDS struck down many men in the 1980s. How could this debilitating and deadly disease be cured and the increasing epidemic curbed? Much effort went into diagnosing and finding drugs to treat those infected. But many deaths ensued and, rather than this disease being a warning to individuals practicing same-sex fornication, HIV/AIDS became a rallying point for sympathy and support. The homosexual activist movement gained political power by calling all opposition homophobic and discriminatory. Indeed they gained much power through drawing sympathy for the consequences of their sexual behavior as they played the victim role.

Of course there was much sympathy as many infected men were truly (self-inflicted) victims of this horrendous disease and suffered greatly. Initially they had no idea that their sexual activity would result in such pain, suffering, and death. Yet many did not want to face the fact that their same-sex activities were the primary cause of the disease and therefore pointed to heterosexuals with the same disease transmitted through the blood. Indeed, heterosexuals were also being infected through receiving blood transfusions from donors with HIV/AIDS. Interestingly, homosexual activists objected to what they believed was anti-gay discrimination, when qualifications for donating blood included being HIV/AIDS free. Thus, for some time innocent recipients of tainted blood transfusions became infected as well, which made it seem as though HIV/AIDS was not a disease limited to homosexual and bi-sexual men.[24] Even though much has been done to help those with HIV/AIDS, Dr. Wu Zunyou, director of China CDC's AIDS-Prevention Center, declared, "No country in the world has discovered an effective way to curb the epidemic among gay men."[25]

Viruses can be deadly and new ones come along. Although Centers for Disease Control and Prevention work assiduously at recommending and facilitating vaccinations for known diseases, they will be unprepared for new ones emerging or those that become antibiotic resistant. The world was unprepared for the Spanish Flu, which was probably the most devastating pandemic the world has yet known:

> The influenza or flu pandemic of 1918 to 1919, the deadliest in modern history, infected an estimated 500 million people worldwide—about one-third of the planet's population at the time—and killed an estimated 20 million to 50 million victims. More than 25 percent of the U.S. population became sick, and some 675,000 Americans died during the pandemic.[26]

Today, in a world of affluence with more people traveling long distances by ground, sea, and air, a lethal new flu strain could spread even more rapidly than the Spanish flu a century ago. One means of a rapid worldwide spread of a new flu virus could be sexual activity and, particularly, oral and anal sex. As Louis Pasteur once warned, "Gentlemen, it is the microbes who will have the last word."

Today, with expanding research in biochemistry, proteins can even be altered. New forms of deadly diseases could be in the making even while experiments are being made for health-giving purposes. We live in the midst of millions of microbes both on the inside and outside of our bodies. Could some of these be altered accidentally? God created men and women with extremely complex systems interacting within each person and with every "foreign" element inside and outside the body. Although much is known about the human body, far more is concealed. Moreover, there is constant change within the body as new cells replace old cells; as food is ingested, digested, and eliminated; as numerous airborne microbes and other contaminants are inhaled along with oxygen; and as airborne microbes are exhaled along with carbon monoxide.

God gave sanitary laws, food laws, and sexually related laws to Israel, many of which worked to prevent many of the diseases of the nations around them. God gave these laws to protect the nation through which the promised Savior would come. For example, in Israel, the laws included exact laws for cleansing after touching a dead body. Throughout the centuries, other nations experienced a high infant mortality rate. Then, in the

1800s, Ignaz Semmelweis in Austria and Oliver Wendell Holmes the U.S. began to recommend hand-washing to prevent disease transmission in hospitals. They particularly noted that when a doctor had performed an autopsy prior to delivering a baby, death ensued.[27]

This is just one of the many discoveries that point to wisdom in the Bible regarding health and safety. God's laws for Israel were not just laws for obedience sake. These were laws for health and safety sake, to protect them from the diseases of the pagan nations around them. **Therefore, we conclude that, because sodomy violates God's sacred sexual design, oral and anal sex, whether indulged in by homosexuals or heterosexuals, could be the cauldron for another worldwide epidemic.**

"Doomsday Clock"

The "Doomsday Clock" has been on every cover of the *Bulletin of the Atomic Scientists* since1947. The concern at first was the annihilation of the world through atomic warfare, but later on other concerns were added, such as climate change, international politics, biotechnology, and other emerging technologies. Since its inception the "Doomsday Clock" has had the minute hand just minutes before midnight, which signifies the moment of global catastrophe and the end of the civilization as we know it.[28] The minute hand has moved back and forth over the years from 2 minutes in 1953 to 17 minutes in 1991 to 3 minutes in 2016 to 2 ½ minutes in 2017.[29] Interestingly, these scientists are only looking at physical and political evidence—not Scripture. They keep changing the clock by observing what's going on in the world.

With the threat of wars, hurricanes, tornadoes, earthquakes and diseases all around us, no one can say exactly what might happen at any given time. However, we do know that earthquakes and floods damage sanitation systems. Without sanitation, viruses and bacteria can spread rapidly through vast areas. There could be a multiplicity of diseases, and, although many of these diseases may not be solely sexually transmitted, those caused by viruses and bacteria in the mouth or anus could easily be transmitted through sodomy. **In fact oral and anal sex could be the primary pathway for the next pandemic to infect and annihilate much of mankind.** Just as God rained fire and brimstone on Sodom and Gomorrah to cleanse the earth from their abominations, so the day will come when God will intervene with judgement.

> Let no man deceive you with vain words: for because of these things cometh the wrath of God upon the children of disobedience. (Eph. 5:6.)

Can Christians Add Time to the "Doomsday Clock"?

Is there a way to slow down the "clock"? We need to remember God's promise to Israel in 2 Chronicles 7:14:

> If my people, which are called by my name, shall humble themselves, and pray, and seek my face, and turn from their wicked ways; then will I hear from heaven, and will forgive their sin, and will heal their land.

In his Old Testament commentary William MacDonald says of 2 Chronicles 7:

> Verse 14 may very well be the golden text of this entire book. Though originally addressed to the chosen nation of Israel, it has rightly been *applied* to those nations which have a biblical heritage. It is the sure road to restoration and revival for all times. If the conditions are met, the promises are sure of fulfillment [30] (Italics his.)

This promise is to God's people. It calls God's children to "humble themselves, and pray, and seek my face, and turn from their wicked ways." The verse is not a call to save society or to reform unbelievers. It is a call to Christians to "humble themselves"—to examine themselves in the light of God's Word, confess their own sins, and repent. Christians have had great freedom to preach the Gospel, send missionaries overseas with the Gospel, and live peaceful lives in this country.

So much is taken for granted and there seems to be very little fear of the Lord among Christians, as many have adopted the world's ways of thinking and acting. Instead of complaining about the sinfulness of others, Christians need to examine how much of the world is in them and repent. We need to ask, "Am I glorifying God?" in whatever we are doing and to repent on the spot. This is not a one-time prayer. This should be ongoing until all people hear the Gospel or until the Lord returns. Will we, as Christians meet the conditions for a fulfillment of this promise?

8

Love God and Your Spouse

The Bible is all about love. God's love is eternal and more far reaching than anyone can fully know. God demonstrates His love throughout Scripture and in the lives of countless believers. Because of God's love, believers are born again. Their faith is grounded in love, and must continue in God's love, which includes grace, mercy, and truth. However, in the midst of the many distractions of daily life, one can forget God's great love and thereby act independently from God and His love. That is why Paul prayed for believers to know the love of God the Father and of Christ the Son:

> For this cause I bow my knees unto the Father of our Lord Jesus Christ, of whom the whole family in heaven and earth is named, that he would grant you, according to the riches of his glory, to be strengthened with might by his Spirit in the inner man; that Christ may dwell in your hearts by faith; that ye, being rooted and grounded in love, may be able to comprehend with all saints what

> is the breadth, and length, and depth, and height;
> and to know the love of Christ, which passeth
> knowledge, that ye might be filled with all the
> fulness of God. (Eph. 3:14-19.)

Believers are enabled to love God by His great love for them: "We love him, because he first loved us" (1 John 4:19). Human love for God is actually in response to His love expressed in so many different ways, but particularly through Christ's substitutionary death on the cross, whereby believers are justified before God and given new life. By means of this new life believers are able to know God, to communicate with Him, and also to trust and obey Him. God is the initiator; Christians are those who respond in faith, love, trust, and obedience. Every commandment is built upon God's love and what God has already done for His children.

In love, God created mankind for a relationship with Himself and with each other. In love He communicated instructions for loving Him and loving one another. When asked what was the greatest of all God's commandments, Jesus answered:

> And thou shalt love the Lord thy God with all
> thy heart, and with all thy soul, and with all thy
> mind, and with all thy strength: this is the first
> commandment. And the second is like, namely
> this, Thou shalt love thy neighbour as thyself."
> (Mark 12:30-31.)

Jesus later commanded His disciples to "love one another, as I have loved you" (John 15:12). Just as Jesus sacrificed Himself to provide salvation for those who believe in Him, He asks His disciples to love sacrificiall .

All sin comes from the failure to love according to God's Word. Self-love will always interfere with love for God, love for one's spouse, and love for others. In His message to the Ephesian church in Revelation, Christ commends them for what they were doing right, but then He says: "Nevertheless I have somewhat against thee, because thou hast left thy first love" (Rev. 2:4). This cooling of love is no light thing, for Jesus then says: "Remember therefore from whence thou art fallen, and repent, and do the first works; or else I will come unto thee quickly, and will remove thy candlestick out of his place, except thou repent" (Rev. 2:5).

Christians might forget the supreme significance of love. Love, whatever direction it goes—to God, spouse, and others, or to self—is the most powerful and deepest human motivation there is. Love can be a strong motivating factor in repentance and obedience. However, if the love is primarily directed towards self, it can fuel inordinate desire, disobedience, and dislike for what is right and good.

Love for God and one another is to be the identifying mark of a Christian, just as love is the defining quality of God, as "God is love" (1 John 4:8, 16). 1 Corinthians 13:4-7 describes what love should look like:

> Charity suffereth long, and is kind; charity envieth not; charity vaunteth not itself, is not puffed up, **doth not behave itself unseemly**, seeketh not her own, is not easily provoked, thinketh no evil; Rejoiceth not in iniquity, but rejoiceth in the truth; Beareth all things, believeth all things, hopeth all things, endureth all things.

Such love is far more than feelings. It involves self-sacrifice and promoting what is good for the other person. When a husband and wife remember and practice this kind of love for one another, they will enjoy far greater intimacy, and their sexual intimacy will be pure as it reflects God's perfect sexual design. Any departure from God's sexual design, however, takes away love, for love "doth not behave itself unseemly, seeketh not her own."

Oral and/or anal sex (which lie within the definitions of fornication and uncleanness) will eat away at their oneness as they are sinning against each other, rather than loving one another. Worse yet, oral and anal sex are violations against God, for sodomy is an abomination, militates against God's sexual design, communicates love for pleasure more than love for God (2 Tim. 3:4), and compromises one's faith to the degree that it may become only a "form of godliness, but denying the power thereof" (2 Tim. 3:4-5).

Christians have been justified and sanctified by the blood of Christ. They are, therefore, holy unto God—set apart for His use in a relationship of love. Therefore, when Christians profane that which is sacred by committing sodomy, they are not only committing the same sensual sins as unbelievers, they are profaning that which is sacred. Those who commit sodomy are directly violating Christ Himself: "Know ye not that your bodies are the members of Christ?" (1 Cor. 6:15). They are like Jerusalem—worse than Sodom—because the inhabitants of Jerusalem multiplied Sodom's abominations (oral and anal sex) (Eze. 16:48-50). After having known God, they turned to idolatry and committed abominations in their idolatry. (Remember that when the word "abomination" is used by itself, it refers to sodomy.[1]) Now in the Twenty-First Century, Christians are bringing sodomy into their marriages and justifying it by misinterpreting the Song of Solomon. (See Chapter 6.) These homosexual practices of oral and anal sex are an abomination to God, and we implore believers, in the name of the Lord of our salvation, to cease and desist.

We began this book with a description of God's sexual design of one man and one woman in a committed relationship of marriage uniting together through coital intercourse for procreation and pleasure. We later revealed how the homosexual oral and anal sexual practices, which are contrary to God's sexual design, proliferated among many heterosexuals, including Christians. **Heterosexuals accepting and practicing oral and/or anal sex became the lynch-pin for all that followed, including the acceptance of the whole homosexual agenda.** We have given biblical and practical reasons why oral and anal sex should **not** be practiced by Christians, but the world, the flesh, and the devil will come against what God would have them do.

Clarion Call to Christian Husbands

This final chapter is a warning and a plea to Christian husbands. From reading sex surveys online, we conclude that it is the husband that pressures the wife into oral and/or anal sex. In doing so, he violates his God-given responsibility to lead his wife in sacrificial love. In drawing his wife into sodomy, he is loving himself more than loving his wife and he is loving pleasure more than loving God (2 Tim. 3:1, 4). We title this chapter "Love

God and Your Spouse" because the husband who loves God and loves his wife according to Scripture will be pleasing God in the marriage bed. In addition, he will be protecting his wife, as well as himself, from the dangers of disease and of deception that can result from sodomy. Because husbands are the initiators and instigators of oral and anal sex, our plea is to Christian husbands to deny themselves such sexual activities for the sake of pleasing God and protecting their wives.

Oral and anal sex are entertained in the minds of many Christian husbands because of various media images and encouragements drenching them with deceitful desires. This fascination is amplified by life-before-marriage, "manly" conversations about sex and further compounded by such media messages as *The Joy of Sex: A Gourmet Guide to Love Making* that promote all kinds of sex, including oral and anal sex.[2]

We live in a sex-saturated society where sexual and sensual appetites have increased voluminously, so much so that the ubiquitous expression "sex sells" is known by virtually everyone. And, the fact is that men think about sex far more and far more differently than women. Add to this the reality of *The Narcissism Epidemic* and the result is an alarming alchemy of sensual and sexual selfism on the part of many men striving for the next sensuous sexual satisfaction.[3] The denouement is a devilish delusion instead of a divine delight.

"Cherchey la femme" is a French expression, which, in English, says, "look for the woman." The phrase is used to convey the idea that a woman is the source of any given problem involving a man. In this case, we say, "Cherchey l'homme." In other words "look for the man." The man is the responsible party in the pursuit of oral and/or anal sex. **Without the husband encouraging his wife to become involved in oral and/or anal sex, it would surely not happen, except for the wife's relational reasons of wanting to love and be loved.** Husbands are biblically called to be the leaders in the home and, therefore, in the sexual relationship. Oral and/or anal sex are not loving, but lustful acts by the husband against his wife and a travesty on God's sexual design.

The penis and vagina are the body parts that unify a husband and wife organically and procreationally as God created them to be one flesh and to multiply upon the earth. Connecting the penis or vagina to other body parts with other purposes degrades and mocks God's design and intent. Oral and anal sex desecrate God's sexual design of coital intercourse and violates the functions and uses of the very body parts involved.

Every time a husband precipitates such a sexual act he defiles God's design and defies God's intent for marriage. Involved in this debasement is the world, the flesh, and the devil. The world produces and promises the "joys of sex," the flesh lusts, and the devil tempts and traps. We trust that Christian husbands truly want to please God, but in the midst of oral and/or anal sex, they are, instead, pleasuring themselves and pleasing the devil. These husbands have been deceived into deriving demonic pleasure from oral and/or anal sex.

By giving heed to the Siren songs of sexual pleasure, many Christian husbands are being seduced to become shipwrecked on the "rocks" of sodomy in their pursuit of sensual gratification. By persuading their wives to enter into such sinful distortions of sexual intercourse, they violate Ephesians 5:25: "Husbands, love your wives, even as Christ also loved the church, and gave himself for it." **Husbands, if you would not express desire and delight in oral or anal sex with your wife, it would never occur!**

The wife is to be in submission to her husband as commanded in Ephesians 5:22: "Wives, submit yourselves unto your own husbands, as unto the Lord." The wife may think she must comply "as unto the Lord," even if the sexual activity is distasteful to her. However, even sex manuals written by and for Christians emphasize that both husband and wife must agree regarding what is done in the marriage bed. Not submitting to unwanted oral and anal sex can be especially difficult for a woman if she desires to please her husband and wants him to love her. She may even choose to be submissive to his sexual desires to keep him from looking elsewhere for gratification. The Christian husband, should never put his wife into such a vulnerable position when he is called to love his wife "even as Christ also loved the church, and gave himself for it" (Eph. 5:25).

Some husbands claim that their wives desire to perform oral sex or participate in anal sex. Some women recognize this as a means of avoiding pregnancy and pleasing their husbands at the same time. What some women will like and do in our sex-laden society should not be copied by Christians. For example, there is a current world-wide, record-setting porn novel, Fifty Shades of Grey, which features erotic scenes of sexual practices that involve BDSM (Bondage, Domination, Submis-sion, Masochism).4 This erotic BDSM porn novel has sold over 125 million copies world-wide and has been translated into 52 languages. According to Bowkers, the agency that issues International Standard Book Numbers (ISBN), eighty percent of those who purchased the book are women. Although it is hard for us to imagine, this no doubt includes many complicit Christian wives, who for some twisted reasons enjoy it. Any Christian man or woman drawn to such sexual perversions needs to seek forgiveness from both God and spouse. Sexual sin dishonors God and corrupts Christian couples.

Until the Lord returns, we will always have psychopathic killers, bank robbers, spousal abusers, and sodomites, but one should not use the exceptions to establish a rule. The Bible clearly reveals that all sexual fornication and uncleanness (including BDSM and sodomy) are not part of God's sexual design, and Christian women need not consent to them. Christian husbands need to protect their wives from all forms of evil. The husband is to love his wife purely and sacrificial y. Husbands are responsible to lead according to God's will. Yet, according to the survey statistics,[5] husbands are the ones who have initiated the egregious error of oral or anal sex. They have, thereby, misused their God-given roles to satisfy themselves in ungodly ways not meant for humankind.

Husbands need to stop pleading or pressuring their wives into oral and/or anal sex. Even the numerous Christians who radically recommend oral and/or anal sex will tell you that a husband should **not** force his wife to submit to either one. **Indeed, out of love, the husband should respect his wife's biblical decision to refuse. We pray that the Holy Spirit will convict those who have been sodomizing their wives and that**

Christian men will set aside their own desires and seek what is pleasing to God.

A husband who has fallen prey to this temptation needs to stop leading his wife down the oral and/or anal sex primrose path of potential pathology (both physical and spiritual). However, because of the intense pleasure husbands derive from oral and anal sex, it will require great effort to withdraw from such sexual satisfaction. The apostle Paul says:

> When Christ, who is our life, shall appear, then shall ye also appear with him in glory. Mortify therefore your members which are upon the earth; fornication, uncleanness, inordinate affection, evil concupiscence, and covetousness, which is idolatry. (Col. 3:4-5.)

"Members" here are body parts, and to "mortify" means to subjugate the bodily passions by abstinence and self-inflicted suffering. Notice that Paul says "mortify," **not** "mollify." In blunt words, Paul is saying to **Stop It!**

Remember that "every man is tempted, when he is drawn away of his own lust, and enticed" (Jas. 1:14). This may be especially difficult for those who have become habituated to the sexual pleasure that comes from dreadful distortions of God's design for sexual intercourse. However, God has given His Word and the Holy Spirit to direct and enable all believers to resist temptation. "Submit yourselves therefore to God. Resist the devil, and he will flee from you" (Jas. 4:7). It may not be easy, but in Christ, such resistance is possible, as well as essential. A Christian man is called to live a life pleasing to God.

Stopping can be especially difficult, because oral and anal sex practices can bring intense pleasure to a man and may be driven by compulsion or ingrained by habitual practice. Nevertheless, Christians need to heed Paul's words to the Thessalonians:

> Furthermore then we beseech you, brethren, and exhort you by the Lord Jesus, that as ye have received of us how ye ought to walk and to please God, so ye would abound more and more. For ye know what commandments we gave you by the Lord Jesus. For this is the will of God, even your sanctification, that ye should **abstain from fornication**: That every one of you should know how to **possess his vessel in sanctification and honour**; Not in the **lust of concupiscence**, even as the Gentiles which know not God: That **no man go beyond and defraud his brother** in any matter: because that the Lord is the avenger of all such, as we also have forewarned you and testified. For **God hath not called us unto uncleanness, but unto holiness**. (1 Thes. 4:1-7, bold added.)

Remember that the word "fornication" encompasses sexual relationships outside marriage and all forms of sexual intercourse that are outside God's created sexual design of coital intercourse.[6] It may be difficult for a man "to possess his vessel in sanctification and honour" after he has indulged in sodomy, but: "There hath no temptation taken you but such as is common to man: but God is faithful, who will not suffer you to be tempted above that ye are able; but will with the temptation also make a way to escape, that ye may be able to bear it" (1 Cor. 10:13).

The words "That no man go beyond and defraud his brother" apply here to the subject of sexual sin. The first application is adultery, but it could also be referring to sodomy. All Christians need to remember and heed the words: "God hath not called us unto uncleanness, but unto holiness." In his letter to the Ephesians, Paul warns:

> But fornication, and all uncleanness, or covetousness, let it not be once named among you, as becometh saints.… Let no man deceive you with vain words: for because of these things cometh the wrath of God upon the children of disobedience.… And have no fellowship with the unfruitful works of darkness, but rather reprove them. For it is a shame even to speak of those things which are done of them in secret. But all things that are reproved are made manifest by the light: for whatsoever doth make manifest is light. (Eph. 5:3, 6, 11-13.)

The Word of God is light and reveals what is pleasing to God and what is dishonoring to both God and man. We pray that Christian husbands will recognize that what they may have been doing, even perhaps in ignorance, is not pleasing to God. Nevertheless, those who are "lovers of pleasures more than lovers of God" (2 Tim. 3:4) will continue to deny that oral and anal sex are wrong as long as it is done between a husband and wife. After all, they can say that there is no specific command against oral and anal sex, only general commands against fornication and uncleanness. But, as we demonstrated in Chapter 5, that argument from silence does not hold. And, if men who love oral and anal sex are not quite sure about what's right, they may rationalize every time they succumb to the temptation, having been "drawn away of [their] own lust, and enticed" (James 1:14).

Depravity involves fallen man's relationship to God. *The Evangelical Dictionary of Theology* states:

> Positively, *total* depravity means that the corruption has extended to all aspects of man's nature, to his entire being; and total *depravity* means that because of that corruption there is nothing man can do to merit saving favor with God.[7] (Italics in original.)

Two of many well-known verses expressing man's heart and lack of righteousness are Jeremiah 17:9 and Isaiah 64:6.

> The heart is deceitful above all things, and desperately wicked: who can know it? (Jer. 17:9.)

> But we are all as an unclean thing, and all our righteousnesses are as filthy rags; and we all do fade as a leaf; and our iniquities, like the wind, have taken us away. (Isaiah 64:6.)

It is with the biblical understanding of our human depravity that we approach the needed change in the sex lives of many Christian couples who are involved in oral and/or anal sex. It is self-evident that the more intense and pleasurable an activity, the more difficult it will be to withdraw from it, especially if it has been indulged in for a long period of time. The longer the period of time and the more regular repetition of oral and/or anal sex, the harder it will be to stop. **It is axiomatic that, if one is in error in one major teaching of the Bible, other errors will follow.**

Satan will come against God's sexual design and ask the same question he asked Eve in the Garden: "Ye, hath God said?" Stopping oral and/or anal sex will be the highest hurdle to get over for those husbands who have been enjoying it and have become habituated to it. Moreover, a plethora of voices from believers have rationalized and justified both oral and anal sex and have misused Scripture with confidence to support what they believe is God's sexual design for the marriage bed. (See Chapter 5.)

Many will not receive the message of this book and many who read a little or a lot of it will more adamantly and immovably believe they have biblical rights to as much oral and/or anal sex as they please. However, **our prayers are that, in spite of those husbands who are submitted and committed to the practice of oral and/or anal sex, some will humbly be able to ask and answer the traditional orthodox question, "Where is that in the Bible?"**

From Sodomy to Spiritual Deception

In addition to dishonoring God and one's spouse, the sin of sodomy can lead to disease and deception. (See Chapter 7.) Throughout much of the Old Testament, God warned Israel and pleaded with her not to intermingle with the nations around them. All of these nations were idolatrous and sexually permissive. Their idolatry included sodomy in the worship of false gods, who were actually demons. As Christians adjust their beliefs to accommodate practicing sodomy, they place themselves in a position of enmity against God and, therefore, make themselves vulnerable to doctrines of demons. Cognitive dissonance, which occurs when a person's belief and practice do not coincide, makes the person feel uncomfortable. Thus to gain a sense of peace, the person changes either the belief or the practice. Too often the behavior wins and the belief is adjusted or scratched to accommodate the chosen behavior. Along the way there is self-justification and a searing of the conscience. Thus, the increase of sodomy among Christians could indeed open them to the deception described in 1 Timothy 4:1-2:

> Now the Spirit speaketh expressly, that in the latter times some shall depart from the faith, giving heed to seducing spirits, and doctrines of devils; Speaking lies in hypocrisy; having their conscience seared with a hot iron.

This will be a form of idolatry: the worship of self—to the degree that: "when they knew God, they glorified him not as God, neither were thankful; but became vain in their imaginations, and their foolish heart was darkened" (Romans 1:21). As Christians move away from knowing and obeying God's Word, they will believe a lie.

Idol worship in the Old Testament included much sexual pleasure through temple prostitutes of both sexes for both sexes. Sex outside marriage and same-sex sexual orgies were part and parcel of idolatrous worship. Thus, as Paul points out in Romans 1, the people were worshipping the creature more than the Creator and indulging in all sorts of unclean sexuality. Although this passage is generally understood to apply to homosexuals, the passage would include oral and anal sex. Since homosexuals cannot engage in coital sex with each other, they corrupt God's sexual design by misusing their God-created bodily parts in ways never intended by God and in ways that demean and mock His design. When heterosexuals, who have the ability to engage in coital intercourse, adopt the sexual practices of homosexuals, they, too, are guilty of uncleanness and fornication, as they violate God's sexual design and intent. Therefore, all individuals who violate God's design through sodomy are included in Romans 1:24-25:

> Wherefore God also gave them up to **uncleanness** through the **lusts of their own hearts**, to **dishonour their own bodies** between themselves: Who changed the truth of God into a lie, and worshipped and served the creature more than the Creator, who is blessed for ever. Amen. (Bold added.)

The "truth of God" is in His creation as well as in His Word. When individuals adjust their beliefs in such a way as to go against nature, that is, against God's creation, they are serving themselves more than serving God. When Christians couples engage in sodomy (oral or anal sex), they are doing the same thing as homosexuals are doing, except with each other. Sodomy contaminating the marriage bed is fornication, which opens the door to further disobedience and further adjustment of beliefs.

Consistency would dictate that those practicing these pagan-like sexual acts could become compromised in their beliefs. Instead of worshipping God, they may be satisfying themselves through the most pernicious, permissive, and pervasive form of idolatry that has ever existed: self-worship. Those who have not kept their sexual garments clean will be exceedingly vulnerable to that deception because they have already been deceiving themselves by justifying their God-dishonoring sexual behavior.

God Is Love and Forgives Sinners

Christians have been given new life in Christ, but they still sin when they walk according to the flesh rather than according to the Spirit. Yet at any moment they have the opportunity to confess (admit they are sinning) and repent (turn around and do what's right).

> But if we walk in the light, as he is in the light, we have fellowship one with another, and the blood of Jesus Christ his Son cleanseth us from all sin. If we say that we have no sin, we deceive ourselves, and the truth is not in us. If we confess our sins, he is faithful and just to forgive us our sins, and to cleanse us from all unrighteousness. If we say that we have not sinned, we make him a liar, and his word is not in us. (1 John 1:9-10.)

God, who loved us while we were yet sinners and gave us new life in Christ (Eph. 2:4-9), continues to love us and continues His work in us through His Word and through His Spirit in the fellowship of like-minded believers. God knows our inner life and uses His Word to reveal and make changes:

> For the word of God is quick, and powerful, and sharper than any twoedged sword, piercing even to the dividing asunder of soul and spirit, and of the joints and marrow, and is a discerner of the

thoughts and intents of the heart. Neither is there any creature that is not manifest in his sight: but all things are naked and opened unto the eyes of him with whom we have to do. (Heb. 4:12-13.)

In addition to revealing sin through His Word, God forgives through His mercy and grace and gives instructions for living a life pleasing to Him:

All scripture is given by inspiration of God, and is profitable for doctrine, for reproof, for correction, for instruction in righteousness: That the man of God may be perfect, throughly furnished unto all good works." (2 Tim. 3:16-17.)

Moreover, believers have an advocate in heaven: Jesus, our Great High Priest, who intercedes for believers who are struggling with temptation:

Seeing then that we have a great high priest, that is passed into the heavens, Jesus the Son of God, let us hold fast our profession. For we have not an high priest which cannot be touched with the feeling of our infirmities; but was in all points tempted like as we are, yet without sin. Let us therefore come boldly unto the throne of grace, that we may obtain mercy, and find grace to help in time of need. (Heb, 4:14-16.)

May every Christian who has been caught in the web of deception and indulged in sodomy (oral and/ or anal sex) repent!

That ye put off concerning the former conversation the old man, which is corrupt according to the deceitful lusts; and be renewed in the spirit of your mind; And that ye put on the new man, which after God is created in righteousness and true holiness. (Eph. 4:22-24.)

Turn away from the world, the flesh, and the devil, and return to the beauty and intimacy of God's sexual design: coital intercourse between one man and one woman within the union of marriage.

End Notes

Introduction

1   "Sodomy," www.legaldictionary.net/sodomy/.

2   Kevin DeYoung. *What Does the Bible Really Teach about Homosexuality?* Wheaton. IL: Crossway, 2015.

3   Martin and Deidre Bobgan, "Dr. Mark Yarhouse's Transgenderized Christianity," *PsychoHeresy Awareness Letter*, Vol. 24, No. 2, http://www.pamweb.org/transgenderized.html.

Chapter 1: God's Sexual Design

1   Janet Raloff, "Chemicals from Plastics Show Effects in Boys," *Science News*, Vol. 176, No. 13, p. 10.

2   "The Neural Roots of Intelligence," *Scientific American Mind*, Vol. 20, No. 6, p. 30.

3   Larry Cahill, "His Brain, Her Brain," *Scientific American*, Vol. 29, No. 5, p. 40.

4   *Ibid.*, p. 41.

5   Louann Brizendine. *The Female Brain.* New York: Morgan Road Books, 2006, inside jacket cover.

6   Cristof Koch, "Regaining the Rainbow," *Scientific American Mind*, Vol. 21, No. 2, p. 16.

7   Amanda MacMillan, "5 Surprising Ways Men and Women Sense Things Differently," 3/26/2015, http://www.health.com/mind-body/5-surprising-ways-men-and-women-sense-things-differently.

8   Kevin DeYoung. *What Does the Bible Really Teach about Homosexuality?* Wheaton. IL: Crossway, 2015, p. 31.

9   *Ibid.*

10   *Ibid.*, p. 32.

11   C. H. Mackintosh. *Notes on the Pentateuch.* Neptune, NJ: Loizeaux Brothers, 1880, 1972, pp 28-29.

12   "Is anal sex ok between a married Christian couple as foreplay?" http://catholicbridge.com/catholic/is_anal_sex_ok_for_married_couples_as_foreplay_catholics.php.

13   William Blackstone, *Commentaries on the Laws of England,* in Blackstone's *Commentaries with Notes of Reference to the Constitution and Laws of the Federal Government of the United States and of the Commonwealth of Virginia,* 5 vols., ed., St. George Tucker. Philadelphia, PA: William Young Birch and Abraham Small, 1803; reprint, South Hackensack, NJ: Rothman Reprints, 1969, 1:38–9. Quoted in "Christianity and Natural and Biblical Law," All About Worldview, http://www.allaboutworldview.org/christianity-and-natural-and-biblical-law-faq.htm#.

14   Walter Bauer. *A Greek-English Lexicon of the New Testament and Other Early Christian Literature,* trans. By William F. Arndt and F. Wilbur Gingrich. Clicago: The University of Chicago Press, 1957, 1979, p.440.

15   *Online Etymology Dictionary,* www.etymonline.com/index.php?term=coitus.

16   J. T. Mueller, "Fornication" in Walter A. Elwell, Ed. *Evangelical Dictionary of Theology,* Second Ed. Grand Rapids, MI: Baker Academic,2001, p.462.

Chapter 2: The Biblical View of Homosexuality

1   E. K. Simpson and F. F. Bruce. *Commentary on the Epistles to the Ephesians and the Colossians.* Grand Rapids, MI: Wm. B. Eerdmans Publishing, 1957, 1975, p. 121

2   "Sodomy," www.legaldictionary.net/sodomy/.

3   "Oral sex," www.nhs.uk.

4   "Anal sex," www.en.wikipedia.org, 5/30/17.

5   "Homosexual," www.google.com.

6   "Activism," www.merriam-webster.com.

7   "Activist," www.dictionary.com.

8   "Revisionism," www.thefreedictionary.com.

9   Kevin DeYoung. *What Does the Bible Really Teach about Homose xuality?* Wheaton. IL" Crossway, 2015.

10   Allen P. Ross. Genesis. In J. F. Walvoord & R. B. Zuck (Eds.), *The Bible Knowledge Commentary: An Exposition of the Scriptures* (Vol. 1, p. 60). Wheaton, IL: Victor Books, 1985, p. 60.

11   Kurt Strassner. *Opening up Genesis*. Leominster, MA: Day One Publications. 2009, p. 83.

12   O. R. Adams. As We Sodomize America: *The Homosexual Movement and the Decline of Morality in America*. Enumclaw, WA: WinePress Publishing, 1998, 2001, p, 217.

13   1 Timothy 1:10, *Adam Clark's Commentary on the Bible* and *John Gill's Exposition of the Entire Bible*, eSword, Version 9.9.1.

14   Warren W. Wiersbe. *Be Holy*. Wheaton, IL: Victor Books, 1996, p. 82.

15   *Ibid.*

16   Matthew Henry, M. *Matthew Henry's Commentary on the Whole Bible: Complete and Unabridged in One Volume*. Peabody, MA: Hendrickson, 1994, p. 172.

17   DeYoung, *op. cit.*, pp. 35-36.

18   Andrew Knowles. *The Bible Guide*. Minneapolis, MN: Augsburg, 2001, p. 74.

19   *Ibid.*, p. 72.

20   G. J. Wenham, "Clean and Unclean" in *New Bible dictionary* (3rd Ed), D. R. W. Wood, I. H. Marshall, A. R. Millard, J. I. Packer, & D. J. Wiseman (Eds.). Leicester, England: Downers Grove, IL::InterVarsity Press, 1996, p. 211.

21   John Gill. *Exposition of the Entire Bible*, eSword.com.

22   Henry, *op. cit.*, p. 2315.

23   "Number of Abortions—Abortion Counters," www.abortion-counters.com, 10/212017.

24   William MacDonald. *Believer's Bible Commentary: Old and New Testaments*, A. Farstad, Ed. Nashville: Thomas Nelson, 1995, p. 1679.

25   Gail Labovitz, "Same-Sex Marriage," Sexual Ethics Project, https://www.brandeis.edu/projects/fse/judaism/docs/essays/same-sex-marriage.pdf.

26   "Timeline of LGBT History," en.widipedia.org, 6/23/17.

27   Vern L. Bullough. *Sexual Variance in Society and History*. Chicago, IL: University of Chicago Press, 1976, 1980, p. 67.

28   *Ibid.*, p. 179.

29   *Ibid.*, pp. 179-180.

30   Louis Crompton. *Homosexuality & Civilization*. Cambridge, MA: The Belknap Press of Harvard University Press, 2003, p. 114.

31   J. A. Witmer. "Romans," in *The Bible Knowledge Commentary: An Exposition of the Scriptures* (Vol. 2). J. F. Walvoord & R. B. Zuck (Eds.). Wheaton, IL: Victor Books, 1985, pp. 443-444.

32   Lawrence S. Mayer and Dr. Paul R. McHugh, "Sexuality and Gender: Findings from the Biological, Psychological, and Social Sciences," *The New Atlantis* Special Report, www.thenewatlantis.com.

33   Ryan T. Anderson, "Almost Everything the Media Tell You About Sexual Orientation and Gender Identity Is Wrong," *The Daily Signal*, August 22, 2016, http://dailysignal.com.

34   Mayer and McHugh, "Executive Summary," "Sexuality and Gender: Findings from the Biological, Psychological, and Social Sciences," *op. cit.*

35   Laurie Higgins, "Homosexuals Admit 'Sexual Orientation' Can and Does Change," Illinois Family Institute, https://illinoisfamily.org/homosexuality/homosexuals-admit-sexual-orientation-can-and-does-change/, 8/12/2017.

36   Camille Paglia in *ibid*.

37   Jane Ward, "No One is Born Gay (or Straight): Here Are 5 Reasons Why," Social (In)Queery, 3/19/2013, https://socialinqueery.com/2013/03/18/no-one-is-born-gay-or-straight-here-are-5-reasons-why/.

38   Trudy Ring, "Exploring the Umbrella: Bisexuality and Fluidity," *The Advocate*, 2/11/2014, https://www.advocate.com/health/love-and-sex/2014/02/11/exploring-umbrella-bisexuality-and-flui -ity.

39   Rosaria Butterfield, "Love Your Neighbor Enough to Speak Truth: A Response to Jen Hatmaker," *The Gospel Coalition*, October 31, 2016, https://www.thegospelcoalition.org/article/love-your-neighbor-enough-to-speak-truth.

40   Rosaria Butterfield. *The Secret Thoughts of an Unlikely Convert*, Expanded Edition. Pennsylvania: Crown & Covenant Publications, 2014, Kindle Edition, Kindle location 691-693.

Chapter 3: The Sexual Revolution

1   Joyce Milton. *The Road to Malpsychia: Humanistic Psychology and Our Discontents*. San Francisco: Encounter Books, 2002, p. 8.

2   *Ibid.*, p. 9.

3   Sigmund Freud. "Sexuality in the Aetiology of the Neuroses" *(1898)* in *Collected Papers,* Volume One. New York: Basic Books, Inc., 1959, p. 220.

4   Sigmund Freud. The Origins of Psychoanalysis: Letters, Drafts and Notes to Wilhelm Fliess (1887-1902). Garden City: Anchor Books, 1957, p. 67.

5   E. M. Thornton, *The Freudian Fallacy.* Garden City: The Dial Press, Doubleday and Company, 1984, p. ix.

6   *Ibid.*, p. 10.

7   "Cultural Relativism," Wikipedia, https://en.wikipedia.org/wili/Cultural_relativism, 8-11-2017.

8   *Ibid.*, p. 12.

9   Milton, op. cit., pp. 16ff.

10   *Ibid.*, pp. 29-30.

11   *Ibid.*, pp. 23-25. 31.

12   *Ibid.*, p. 39.

13   *Ibid.*

14   *Ibid.* pp. 17-21.

15   Ruth Benedict, "Anthropology and the Abnormal," *Journal of General Psychology*, Vol. 10, No. 2, pp. 59-82.

16   Milton, *op. cit.* p. 39.

17   *Ibid.*, p. 55.

18   Adrianne Aron, "Maslow's Other Child" in *Politics and Innocence,* Rollo May, Carl Rogers, Abraham Maslow et al., eds. Dallas: Saybrook Publishers, 1986, p. 96.

19   Ayn Rand. *The Virtue of Selfishness.* New York: Penguin, 1964, p. ix.

20   Anne C. Heller. *Ayn Rand and the World She Made.* New York: Doubleday, 2009, p. 411.

21   Nathaniel Branden. *The Psychology of Self-Esteem*. Danvers, MA: Josey-Bass, 1969, 2001.

22   Nathaniel Branden. *Honoring the Self: Self-Esteem and Personal Transformation*. New York: Bantam Books, 1983, 1985.

23   Daniel Yankelovich. *New Rules: Searching for Self-Fulfillment in a World Turned Upside Down*. New York: Random House, 1981, p. xviii.

24   Charles Reich. *The Greening of America*. New York:; Bantam Books, 1971, p. 9.

25   Jerry Bergman, "Kinsey, Darwin, and the Sexual Revolution," Creation Ministries International, https://creation.com/kinsey-darwin-and-the-sexual-revolution.

26   Alfred Charles Kinsey, Wardell B. Pomeroy, Clyde E. Martin. *Sexual Behavior in the Human Male*, Philadelphia,PA: W. B. Saunders, 1948.

27   Alfred Charles Kinsey, Wardell B. Pomeroy, Clyde E. Martin. *Sexual Behavior in the Human Female*. Philadelphia,PA: W. B. Saunders, 1953.

28   "Alfred Kinsey," Wikipedia, referencing James H. Jones. *Alfred C. Kinsey: A Life*. New York: W. W. Norton & Company, 2004, p. 610.

29   "Alfred Kinsey," Wikipedia, referencing David J. Ley. *Insatiable Wives: Women Who Stray and the Men Who Love Them*. Lanham, MD: Rowman & Littlefield, 2009, p. 59

30   Paul Cameron, "How Many Homosexuals Are There?" Family Research Institute, http://www.familyresearchinst.org/2012/01/how-many-homosexuals-are-there/.

31   Vern L. Bulluogh. *Sexual Variance in Society and History*. Chicago: University of Chicago Press, 1976, p. 25.

32   *Ibid.*, p. 2.

33   Cameron, *op. cit.*

34   Alfred C. Kinsey, Wardell B. Pomeroy, Clyde E. Martin, and Paul H. Gebhard, "Concepts of Normality and Abnormality in Sexual Behavior" in *Psychosexual Development in Health and Disease*, Paul H. Hoch and Joseph Zubin, eds., New York: Grune & Stratton, 1949, p. 14.

35   Kinsey et al. Ibid., p. 16.

36   Kinsey et al. Ibid., p. 23.

37   Kinsey et al. Ibid., p. 32.

38   Judith A. Reisman and Edward W. Eichel. *Kinsey, Sex and Fraud: The Indoctrination of a People.* Lafayette, LA: Lochinvar-Huntington House, 1990, p. 2; http://www.drjudithreisman.com/archives/Kinsey_Sex_and_Fraud.pdf.

39   Nancy L. Cohen, "How the Sexual Revolution Changed America Forever," Alternet, http://www.alternet.org/story/153969/how_the_sexual_revolution_changed_america_forever.

40   "Combined oral contraceptive pill," Wikipedia, https://en.wikipedia.org/wiki/Combined_oral_contraceptive_pill#cite_note-tone-9, 8-11-17.

41   "Sexual Revolution in the 1960s United States," Wikipedia, https://en.wikipedia.org/wiki/Sexual_revolution_in_1960s_United_States, 6/14/17.

42   "Roe v. Wade," Wikipedia, https://en.wikipedia.org/wiki/Roe_v._Wade, 9-10-2017.

43   "Sexual Revolution in the 1960s United States," Wikipedia, *op. cit.*

44   "Sodomy Laws in the United States," Wikipedia, https://en.wikipedia.org/wiki/Sodomy_laws_in_the_United_States.

45   *The American Journal of Psychiatry*, "The diagnostic status of homosexuality in DSM-III: a reformulation of the issues," Volume 138 Issue 2, February 1981, pp. 210-215, Abstract at http://ajp.psychiatryonline.org/doi/abs/10.1176/ajp.138.2.210.

46   Hunter Stuart, "Not All Pedophiles Have Mental Disorder, American Psychiatric Association Says in New DSM," *Huffington Post*, Nov. 1, 2013,

47   "Sexual Revolution in the 1960s United States," *op. cit.*

48   "Sexual Revolution," Wikipedia, https://en.wikipedia.org/wiki/Sexual_revolution, 5/4/2017.

Chapter 4: The Sodomy of Americans

1   Eva S. Moskowitz. *In Therapy We Trust: America's Obsession with Self-Fulfillment.* Baltimore: The Johns Hopkins University Press, 2001, pp. 2-3.

2   Christina Hoff Sommers and Sally Satel. *One Nation Under Therapy: How the Helping Culture Is Eroding Self-Reliance*. New York: St. Martin's Press, 2005, inside book cover.

3   Jean M. Twenge and W. Keith Campbell. *The Narcissism Epidemic: Living in an Age of Entitlement*. New York: Free Press, 2009, 2010, p. xii.

4   *Ibid.*, p. 308.

5   *Ibid.*, p. x.

6   "Timeline of LGBT History," en.wikipedia.org, 6/23/17.

7   "History of Homosexuality," https://en.wikipedia.org/wiki/History_of_homosexuality, 6/15/17.

8   O. R. Adams. *As We Sodomize America: The Homosexual Movement and the Decline of Morality in America*. Emunclaw, WA: Winepress Publishing, 1998, 2001, p. 27.

9   . "Oral Sex," *Wikipedia*, 9/16/2016, https://en.wikipedia.org/wiki/Oral_sex.

10   Paul Cameron, "Medical Consequences of What Homosexuals Do," Family Research Institute, http://www.familyresearchinst.org/2009/02/medical-consequences-of-what-homosexuals-do/.

11   Ligonier Ministries, "The State of Theology: Theological Awareness Benchmark Study," *Research Report*, Ligonier Ministries, 10/24/2014, p. 4.

12   O. R. Adams, Jr., "As We Sodomize Our Churches," http://www.americantraditions.org/Articles/The%20Sodomizing%20of%20Our%20Churches.htm.

13   "Ashley Madison," https://en.wikipedia.org/wiki/Ashley_Madison.

14   Anjani Chandra, *et al.*, "Sexual Behavior, Sexual Attraction, and Sexual Identity in the United States: Data from 2006-2008 National Survey of Family Growth," National Health Statistics Reports, Number 36, 3/3/2011.

15   "Americans More Accepting of Gay Relationships, Less Comfortable with Divorce," Associated Press, March 17, 2016, www.foxnews.com.

16   Linda Mintle, "Pornography and the Brain," *Christian Counseling Today*, Vol. 22, No. 1, p. 19.

17   Mary Sykes Wylie, "The Unspeakable Language of Sex," *Psychotherapy Networker*, Vol. 40, No. 1, p. 16.

18   "Pornography Addiction Statistics," https://www.xxxchurch.com/pornography-addiction-statistics.

19   Donald L. Hilton, Jr. and Clark Watts, "Pornography Addiction: A Neuroscience Perspective, *Surgical Neurology International*, 2/19/2011, https://www.ncbi.nlm.nih.gov/pmc/articles/PMC3050060/.

20   Judith Reisman. *Sexual Sabotage: How One Mad Scientist Unleashed a Plague of Corruption and Contagion in America*. Washington, DC: WND Books, 2010, p. 188.

21   Siecus, http://www.siecus.org/index.cfm?fuseaction=Page.viewPage&pageId=493.

22   "Psycho-Sexual Development," quoted in *Planned Parenthood News*, Summer 1953, p. 10, https://www.cnsnews.com/blog/jim-sedlak/why-are-people-so-mad-planned-parenthood.

23   Reisman, *op. cit.*, pp. 188-199.

24   "Resources for Parents," Planned Parenthood, https://www.plannedparenthood.org/learn/parents/resources-parents.

25   Renee Nal, "Report: Chicago schools teaching 'safe' anal sex to 5th graders," Education Action Group Foundation, Inc., http://eagnews.org/report-chicago-schools-teaching-safe-anal-sex-to-5th-graders/.

26   Todd Starnes, "Parents outraged over *Teen Vogue* anal sex how-to column (but magazine still defends it), Fox News, 7/18/2017, http://www.foxnews.com/opinion/2017/07/18/teen-vogue-defends-teaching-kids-how-to-engage-in-sodomy.html.

27   Todd Starnes, "*Teen Vogue* Defends Teaching Kids How to Engage in Sodomy," www.foxnews.com/opinion/2017/07/18/teen-vogue-defends-teaching-kids-how-to-engage-in-sodomy.html.

28   "First Openly Gay Miss Missouri Crowned," Fox News, 6/23/2016, www.foxnews.com.

29   Jean M. Twenge,, Ryne A Sherman, and Brooke E. Wells, "Changes in American Adults' Reported Same-sex Sexual Experiences and Attitudes, 1973-2014," original article in *Archives of Sexual Behavior*, 2016, made available by Springer Science+Business Media New York, 2016, http://link.springer.com/article/10.1007/s10508-016-0769-4.

30   *Ibid.*, p. 16.

31   Ibid., p. 5.

32   *Ibid*, p. 2.

33   *Ibid.,*

34   "Number of Abortions—Abortion Counters," www.abortion-counters.com, 10/21/2017.

35   *The American Journal of Psychiatry*, "The diagnostic status of homosexuality in DSM-III: a reformulation of the issues," Volume 138 Issue 2, February 1981, pp. 210-215, Abstract at http://ajp.psychiatryonline.org/doi/abs/10.1176/ajp.138.2.210.

36   Charles J. Sykes. *A Nation of Victims: The Decay of the American Character*. New York: St. Martin's Press, 1992, p. xiii.

37   *Ibid.*, p. 11.

38   *Ibid.*, pp. 16-17.

39   *Ibid.*, p 17.

40   *Ibid.*, p. 20.

41   Joseph D. Unwin. *Sex and Culture*. London: Oxford University Press, 1934, pp. viii-ix, available as an electronic resource at https://archive.org/details/b20442580.

42   *Ibid.*, p. ix.

43   *Ibid.*, p. 381.

44   *Ibid.*, p. 382.

45   *Ibid.*, p. 365.

46   *Ibid.*, pp. 311-12.

47   Joseph D. Unwin, "Monogamy as a Condition of Social Energy," *The Hibbert Journal*, Vol. XXV, 1927, p. 662.

48   *Ibid.*

Chapter 5: The Sodomy of Christians

1   Ligonier Ministries, "The State of Theology: Theological Awareness Benchmark Study," *Research Report*, Ligonier Ministries, 10/24/2014, p. 4.

2   Barna Group, "The End of Absolutes: America's New Moral Code," 5/25/16, https://www.barna.org/research/culture-media/research-release/americas-new-moral-code#.V4LTeaJWhzs.

3   *Ibid.*

4   *Ibid.*

5   *Ibid.*

6   "Ashley Madison," https://en.wikipedia.org/wiki/Ashley_Madison.

7   Cindy Crosby, "The Best Sex (Survey) Ever!" *Today's Christian Woman*, 2008, http://www.todayschristianwoman.com/articles/2008/september/best-sex-survey-ever.html.

8   *Ibid.*

9   "Pornography" in *Webster's Encyclopedic Unabridged Dictionary of the English Language*. New York: Gramercy Books, 1996, p. 1506.

10   Christiane J. Gardner, "Tangled in the Worst of the Web," *Christianity Today*, March 5, 2001, http://www.christianitytoday.com/ct/2001/march5/1.42.html.

11   "Survey: Alarming rate of Christian men look at porn, commit adultery," https://www.onenewsnow.com/culture/2014/10/09/survey-alarming-rate-of-christian-men-look-at-porn-commit-adultery.

12   "The Porn Phenomenon," Barna Group," https://www.barna.com/the-porn-phenomenon/.

13   Marnie C. Ferree, "Women and Pornography Today," *Christian Counseling Today*, Vol. 22, No. 1, p. 50.

14   "The Porn Phenomenon," *op. cit.*

15   Ferree, *op. cit.*

16   "Most U.S. Christian groups grow more accepting of homosexuality," Pew Research Center, http://www.pewresearch.org/fact-tank/2015/12/18/most-u-s-christian-groups-grow-more-accepting-of-homosexuality/ft_15-12-15_homosexualitychristiangroups/.

17   David Masci and Michael Lipka, "Where Christian churches, other religions stand on gay marriage," Pew Research Center, http://www.pewresearch.org/fact-tank/2015/12/21/where-christian-churches-stand-on-gay-marriage/.

18   Mark Regnerus, "Tracking Christian Sexual Morality in a Same-Sex Marriage Future," *The Witherton Institute Public Discourse*, http://www.thepublicdiscourse.com/2014/08/13667/.

19   Cathy Lynn Grossman, "Survey: Tolerance for gays, lesbians rises rapidly," Religious News Service, Feb. 26, 2014, https://www.usatoday.com/story/news/nation/2014/02/26/homosexuality-opinion-survey/5828455/.

20   Tim and Beverly LaHaye. *The Act of Marriage: The Beauty of Sexual Love*. Grand Rapids, MI: Zondervon Press, 1976.

21   Tim and Beverly LaHaye with Mike Yorkey. *The Act of Marriage after 40: Making Love for Life*. Grand Rapids, MI: Zondervon Press, 2000, p. 262.

22   LaHaye, *The Act of Marriage, op., cit.*, p. 210.

23   *Ibid.*, p. 211.

24   *Ibid.*, p. 295, 296.

25   LaHaye, *The Act of Marriage after 40, op. cit.*, p. 19.

26   *Ibid.*, p. 89.

27   Kevin Leman. *Sheet Music: Uncovering the Secrets of sexual Intimacy in Marriage*. Carol Stream, IL: Tyndale House Publishers, Inc., 2003, 2008.

28   *Ibid.*, p. 166.

29   *Ibid.,* Chapter 6.

30   *Ibid.,* Chapter 5.

31   *Ibid.,* Chapter 7.

32   www.amazon.com.

33   Mark Woods, "Former Mars Hill elder gives inside story of controversial plan to boost Mark Driscoll's book sales," *Christianity Today*, April 23, 2015, https://www.christiantoday.com/article/former.mars.hill.elder.gives.inside.story.of.controversial.plan.to.boost.mark.driscolls.book.sales/52669.htm.

34   Mark and Grace Driscoll. *Real Marriage: The Truth about Sex, Friendship, and Life Together*. Nashville, TN: Thomas Nelson, 2012, p. 177.

35   *Ibid.*, p. 185.

36   *Ibid.*, p. 186.

37   *Ibid.*, p. 187.

38   *Ibid.*

39   *Ibid.*, p. 188.

40   Sodomy, *The Legal Dictionary*, http://legaldictionary.net/sodomy/..

41   Driscolls, *op. cit.*, p. 188.

42   *Ibid.*, p. 189.

43   *Forbes* magazine identifi s Driscoll as "one of the nation's most prominent and celebrated pastors," en.wikipedia.org/wiki/Mark_Driscoll; Rob Asghar, "Mars Hill: Cautionary Tales From The Enron Of American Churches," *Forbes,* September 16, 2014.

44   Ed Wheat and Gaye Wheat. *Intended for Pleasure: Sex Technique and Sexual Fulfillment in Christian Marriage,* 4th Ed. Grand Rapids, MI: Revell, 1977, 1997, Back Cover.

45   *Ibid.,* pp. 241-242.

46   LaHaye, *The Act of Marriage, op., cit.,* p. 89.

47   LaHaye. *The Act of Marriage after 40, op. cit.,* p. 89.

48   Leman. *Sheet Music, op. cit.,* p. 113.

49   Driscoll. *Real Marriage, op. cit,* p. 187.

50   Focus on the Family Daily Broadcast, www.focusonthefamily.com

51   Focus on the Family, "Oral and Anal Sex: Biblical Guidelines for Intimacy in Marriage," https://www.focusonthefamily.com/family-q-and-a/relationships-and-marriage/oral-and-anal-sex-biblical-guidelines-for-intimacy-in-marriage.

52   LaHaye, *The Act of Marriage After Forty, op. cit,* p. 89.

53   Leman, *op. cit.,* p. 166.

54   John Piper, "Interview with John Piper," www.desiringgod.org/interviews/is-oral-sex-okay.

Chapter 6: The Song of Solomon

1   J. Paul Tanner, "The History of Interpretation of the Song of Songs," *Bibliotheca Sacra,* 154: 613, 1997, p. 23, http://paultanner.org/English%20HTML/Publ%20Articles/Hist%20Song%20of%20Songs%20-%20P%20Tanner.pdf.

2   William MacDonald. *Believer's Bible Commentary: Old and New Testaments,* A. Farstad, Ed. Nashville, TN: Thomas Nelson, 1995, p. 919.

3   Franz Delitzsch, "The Song of Songs," in *Biblical Commentary on the Old Testament.* Grand Rapids, MI: Wm B. Eerdmans Publishing Company,1971, Vol 16, p. 1

4   MacDonald, *op. cit.*

5   A. R, Fausset, "Song of Songs," in R. Jamieson, A. R. Fausset, & D. Brown. *Commentary Critical and Explanatory on the Whole*

Bible. Oak Harbor, WA: Logos Research Systems, Inc, 1997, Vol. 1, p. 414.

6   Matthew Henry. *Matthew Henry's Commentary on the Whole Bible: Complete and Unabridged In One Volume*. Peabody, MA: Hendrickson, 1994, pp. 1056–1057.

7   Jack S. Deere, "Song of Songs" in *The Bible Knowledge Commentary: An Exposition of the Scriptures,* J. F. Walvoord & R. B. Zuck, Eds. Wheaton, IL: Victor Books, 1985, Vol. 1, pp. 1008-1010.

8   Mark Driscoll, "Sex, a Study of the Good Bits from Song of Solomon," preached in Edinburgh, Scotland, 11/18/2007.

9   Joseph C. Dillow. *Solomon on Sex*. Nashville: Thomas Nelson, 1982, p. 27.

10   Driscoll, *op. cit.*, p. 186.

11   Dr. Heath Lambert, https://biblicalcounseling.com/about/staff/dr-heath-lambert/.

12   John MacArthur, "The Rape of Solomon's Song," Part 1, www.gty.org.

Chapter 7: Dangers and Diseases of Sodomy

1   Paul Cameron, "Medical Consequences of What Homosexuals Do," Family Research Institute, http://www.familyresearchinst.org/2009/02/medical-consequences-of-what-homosexuals-do/.

2   O. R. Adams. *As We Sodomize America: The Homosexual Movement and the Decline of Morality in America*. Enumclaw, WA: WinePress Publishing, 1998, 2001, pp. 19-65.

3   Lawrence S. Mayer and Dr. Paul R. McHugh, "Sexuality and Gender: Findings from the Biological, Psychological, and Social Sciences," *The New Atlantis* Special Report, www.thenewatlantis.com.

4   Andrew M. Seaman, "Survey Finds Excess Health Problems in Lesbians, Gays, Bisexuals," http://www.reuters.com/article/us-health-lgbt-disparities-idUSKCN0ZE2XE.

5   Lorraine Day. AIDS What the Government Isn't Telling You, Palm Desert, CA: Rockford Press, 1991, pp. 111-112.

6   "Anal sex," www.en.wikipedia.org, 5/30/17.

7   "Anal Sex," Clifford and Joyce Penner, http://passionatecommitment.com/faqs-about-sex/.

8   Marnie C. Ferree, "Women and Pornography Today," *Christian Counseling Today*, Vol. 22, No. 1, p. 51.

9   "Anal Sex Safety and Health Concerns," WebMD, http://www.webmd.com/sex/anal-sex-health-concerns#1.

10   "What Are the Risk Factors for Anal Cancer? American Cancer Society,   www.cancer.org/cancer/anal-cancer/causes-risks-prevention/risk-factors.html.

11   "Anal Sex Safety and Health Concerns," *op. cit.*

12   "Oral sex," www.nhs.uk.

13   Evann E. Hilt, et al., "Urine Is Not Sterile: Techniques To Detect Resident Bacterial Flora in the Adult Female Bladder," *Journal of Clinical Microbiology*," Vol. 52, No. 3, pp. 871-876.

14   Rajiv Saini, et al., "Oral Sex, Oral Health and Orogenital Infections, *Journal of Global Infectious Diseases,* Jan-Apr, 2010, https://www.ncbi.nlm.nih.gov/pmc/articles/PMC2840968/.

15   David Delvin, "Infection Rists Associated with Oral Sex," http://www.netdoctor.co.uk/conditions/sexual-health/a12020/infection-risks-associated-with-oral-sex/.

16   "What Infections Can I Catch Through Oral Sex?" National Health Service, United Kingdom, http://www.nhs.uk/chq/Pages/970.aspx?CategoryID=118.

17   Centers for Disease Control and Prevention, "Human Papilloma Virus (HPV)," https://www.cdc.gov/hpv/?s_cid=PN-NCIRD-Teen-AW-CancerPrevention-HPV_Prevention-8.

18   Centers for Disease Control and Prevention, "Why Is HPV Vaccine So Important," https://www.cdc.gov/hpv/hcp/hpv-important.html.

19   "Reported STDs at Unprecedented High in the U.S.," Centers for Disease Control and Prevention, https://www.cdc.gov/nchhstp/newsroom/2016/std-surveillance-report-2015-press-release.html.

20   Helen Branswell, "Gonorrhea May Become Resistant to All Antibiotics Sooner than Anticipated." *Scientific American*, 9/22/20, https://www.scientificamerican.com/article/gonorrhea-may-b -come-resistant-to-all-antibiotics-sooner-than-anticipated/.

21   Anjani Chandra, *et al.*, "Sexual Behavior, Sexual Attraction, and Sexual Identity in the United States: Data from 2006-2008 National Survey of Family Growth," National Health Statistics Reports, Number 36, 3/3/2011.

22   Centers for Disease Control and Prevention, "Use of a 2-Dose Schedule for Human Papillomavirus Vaccination — Updated Recommendations of the Advisory Committee on Immunization Practices," https://www.cdc.gov/mmwr/volumes/65/wr/mm6549a5.htm.

23   "Global Health Observatory (GHO) data HIV/AIDS," http://www.who.int/gho/hiv/en/.

24   Adams, *op. cit.* 81.

25   Fanfan Wang, "HIV in Gay Men Tests Chinese Respone," *Wall Street Journal*, 9/28/2016, p. A8.

26   "1918 Flu Pandemic," http://www.history.com/topics/1918-flu pandemic.

27   Hilary L.Lane et, et al., "Oliver Wendell Holmes (1809-1894) and Ignaz Philipp Semmelweis (1818-1865): Preventing the Transmission of Puerperal Fever," American Public Health Association, June, 2009, https://www.ncbi.nlm.nih.gov/pmc/articles/PMC2866610/.

28   "Doomsday Clock," Wikipedia, https://en.wikipedia.org/wiki/Doomsday_Clock.

29   "Its Two and a Half Minutes to Midnight," *Bulletin of the Atomic Scientists*, http://thebulletin.org/clock/2017.

30   William MacDonald. *Believer's Bible Commentary: Old and New Testaments*, A. Farstad, Ed. Nashville, TN: Thomas Nelson, 1995, p. 449..

Chapter 8: Love God and Your Spouse

1   DeYoung, Kevin. *What Does the Bible Really Teach about Homosexuality?* Wheaton, IL: Crossway. Kindle Edition, 2015m, pp. 35-36.

2   Alex Comfort. *The Joy of Sex: A Gourmet Guide to Love Making*, New York: Crown, 1972.

3   Jean M. Twenge and W. Keith Campbell. *The Narcissism Epidemic*. New York: Free Press, 2010.

4   E. L. James. *Fifty Shades of Grey*. New York: Vintage Books, 2012.

5   See Chapters 3 through 5.

6   J. T. Mueller, "Fornication" in Walter A. Elwell, Ed. *Evangelical Dictionary of Theology*, Second Ed. Grand Rapids, MI: Baker Academic,2001, p. 462.

7   C. C. Ryrie, "Depravity, Total," in Walter A. Elwell, ed. *Evangelical Dictionary of Theology*, 2nd Ed. Grand Rapids, MI: Baker Academic., 1984, 2001, p. 337.

Visit

www.pamweb.org/mainpage.html

for

free ebooks, articles,

and video links